Using Email on the Internet

A step-by-step guide to sending and receiving messages and files

Internet Handbooks

1001 Web Sites for Writers on the Internet
Books and Publishing on the Internet
Building a Web Site on the Internet
Careers Guidance on the Internet
Chat & Chat Rooms on the Internet
Creating a Home Page on the Internet
Discussion Forums on the Internet
Education & Training on the Internet
Exploring Yahoo! on the Internet
Find It on the Internet
Finding a Job on the Internet
Free Software on the Internet
Free Stuff on the Internet
Getting Connected to the Internet
Getting Started on the Internet
Gardens & Gardening on the Internet
Graduate Job Hunting on the Internet
Homes & Property on the Internet
Human Resource Management on the Internet
Internet Explorer on the Internet
Internet for Schools
Internet for Students
Internet for Writers
Internet Skills for the Workplace
Law & Lawyers on the Internet
Linking Your Web Site on the Internet
Managing the Internet in Your Organisation
Marketing Your Business on the Internet
Music & Musicians on the Internet
Naming a Web Site on the Internet
News and Magazines on the Internet
Overseas Job Hunting on the Internet
Personal Finance on the Internet
Promoting a Web Site on the Internet
Protecting Children on the Internet
Shops & Shopping on the Internet
Studying English on the Internet
Studying Law on the Internet
Travel & Holidays on the Internet
Using Credit Cards on the Internet
Using Email on the Internet
Using Netscape on the Internet
WAP and Cellphones on the Internet
Where to Find It on the Internet
Wildlife & Conservation on the Internet
Working from Home on the Internet
Your Privacy on the Internet

Other titles in preparation

internet
handbooks

Using Email

on the internet

A step-by-step guide to sending and
receiving messages and files

Kye Valongo

www.internet-handbooks.co.uk

Other Internet Handbooks by the same author

Discussion Forums on the Internet
Free Stuff on the Internet
Getting Started on the Internet
Internet Explorer on the Internet
Using Netscape on the Internet
Where to Find It on the Internet

First published in 2001 by Internet Handbooks Ltd, Plymbridge House, Estover Road, Plymouth PL6 7PY, United Kingdom.

Customer services tel:	(01752) 202301
Orders fax:	(01752) 202333
Customer services email:	cservs@plymbridge.com
Distributors web site:	www.plymbridge.com
Internet Handbooks web site:	www.internet-handbooks.co.uk

Note: The contents of this book are offered for the purposes of general guidance only and no liability can be accepted for any loss or expense incurred as a result of relying in particular circumstances on statements made in this book. Readers are advised to check the current position with the appropriate authorities before entering into personal arrangements.

Case studies in this book are entirely fictional and any resemblance to real persons or organisations is entirely coincidental.

Printed and bound by The Cromwell Press Ltd, Trowbridge, Wiltshire.

Contents

List of illustrations   7

Preface   9

1   Fast track: getting started   11

Your email address   11
Your email program   13
Your mail server   15
Writing and reading messages   15
Creating a test message   16
Connect!   17
Sending and receiving your first email message   19
Disconnecting   19
Reading messages   19

2   Sending and replying to emails   21

Finding someone's email address   21
Your email address book   22
Replying to a message   24
Forwarding a message   25
Sending an email to more than one person   26
Formatting your message text   27
Adding graphics to your messages   28
Adding a sound track to your messages   29
More HTML tips   30
When not to use HTML for email messages   31

3   Managing your emails   33

Sorting messages   33
Deleting messages   33
Organising your messages into folders   35
Filtering your incoming emails   36
Filtering emails in Outlook Express   37
Filtering emails in Netscape Messenger   39
Junk email   40
Defending yourself against spam   41
Identifying the sender of an email   42
Where to complain   43
How to view message headers   43
Don't be a spammer   44

4   Sending and receiving files   45

Attaching files to emails   45
Compressing files   46
Compression software   47
Decompressing files   49
Breaking up large messages   49
The threat of viruses   50
Protecting against virus infection   51
Antivirus software   52

Contents

5 Social email   58

Taking part: internet mailing lists   58
Playing games by email   65

6 Your email privacy   67

Your emails at work or college   67
The problem of file deletion   67
Some tips for employees   67
PGP encryption   69
Using anonymous email   72
Using remailers   72
Anonymous web-based email   75

7 Email on the move   76

Web email access   76
Web-based private email   78
Using your existing email mailbox   80
Checking your mail server details   81

8 Anything goes   84

FTP by email   84
The world wide web by email   86
Searching the web by email   87
Usenet by email   88
Reading Usenet newsgroups by email   89
Posting messages in Usenet newsgroups   90
Note on Usenet posting   91
Email to snail mail   91
Sending a fax by email   92
Automatic message translation   93

Appendices: More help with email

1   Essential web sites about email   95
2   Manually configuring your software   97

Glossary of internet terms   101

Index   117

List of illustrations

Figure   *Page*

1. Outlook Express   13
2. Netscape Messenger   16
3. Sending a test message   17
4. Dial up networking: connect   18
5. Dial up networking: minimised   18
6. Dial up networking: connected   18
7. Netscape's View menu   20
8. The Yahoo! email directory   22
9. The Outlook Express address book   23
10. Snipping message quotes   25
11. Outlook Express stationery wizard   27
12. Inserting an image into an email   29
13. HTML formatting in Messenger   31
14. Messages formatted with HTML   32
15. Deleting email in Outlook Express   34
16. Deleting email in Netscape   34
17. Setting message filters and folders   35
18. Creating a folder in Outlook Express   36
19. Creating a folder in Netscape   36
20. Filtering rules in Outlook Express   38
21. Filtering rules in Netscape   39
22. Spam or unsolicited mail   42
23. Network Abuse Clearinghouse   44
24. Outlook Express email attachments   46
25. Netscape Messenger email attachments   47
26. Email composition with attached file   47
27. WinZip: choosing the file to unzip   48
28. WinZip: unzipping   48
29. Breaking up large messages   50
30. Data Rescue   51
31. Dr Solomon's AntiVirus Toolkit   53
32. Download.com for anti-virus software   54
33. Setting Microsoft Word against viruses   55
34. Virus hoaxes   57
35. Liszt for internet mailing lists   59
36. Subscribing to a mailing list   61
37. Email rules or filters   63
38. Unsubscribing from a mailing list   64
39. Email games   66
40. PGP for email encryption   69
41. Ziplip for email encryption   73
42. Zero Knowledge for internet privacy   75
43. Hotmail web-based email   76

Illustrations..

Figure	Page
44. Yahoo! web-based email	77
45. Hushmail for secure email on the move	78
46. ZipLip	79
47. Anonymizer for web-based anonymity	80
48. Web2Mail for PDAs and mobiles	81
49. Your mail server in Outlook Express	82
50. Your mail server in Netscape	83
51. A list of FTPmail servers	88
52. Deja.com for newsgroup messages	89
53. The Phone Company (TPC) for faxes	92
54. T-Mail for email translations	93
55. Setting up a new Dial-Up Networking entry.	97
56. Adding a new email account to Outlook Express.	98

Preface

Email stands for electronic mail. It is electronic because it is sent and received across a telephone system or communications network. Email allows you to exchange messages almost immediately with anyone in the world so long as they have internet access at home, at work, or at a library or internet cafe. Millions of people each day have come to depend on email. They use it to send business information and private messages and share public opinions with others. You can also attach pictures, video clips, sound tracks, and all kinds of other computer files to your email messages, and receive similar files from a sender.

Email is much faster and cheaper than normal mail. An email message sometimes takes literally only a few seconds to reach a destination on the other side of the world. You can send hundreds of email messages before your telephone call charge rises above the five pence minimum.

Email also has several advantages over telephone conversations, as well. Firstly, the person you are communicating with doesn't have to be connected at the same time as you are. If the other person is unavailable, your message will remain on the internet until the other person connects to the internet to retrieve it. Secondly, you can keep and print a copy of all messages sent and received. And, of course, if you are sending messages overseas, the cost of an email message is far lower than an international telephone call.

For many people, email is the only feature of the internet that they ever use but, as you will see later in the book, you can do almost anything by email that can be done on the internet. Indeed, email is the most powerful – and underused – part of the internet. Designed mainly for Windows PC users, this book will show you in easy practical steps how to use email, how to get started quickly, and how to protect yourself from the risks of computer viruses and junk mail.

Learning the valuable skills discussed in the following pages could change your life, whether at home, at leisure, as a student or in the workplace. Go for it!

Kye Valongo
kyevalongo@internet-handbooks.co.uk

1 Fast track: getting started

In this chapter we will explore:

▶ *your email address*
▶ *your email program*
▶ *your mail server*
▶ *writing and reading messages*
▶ *creating a test message*
▶ *connect!*
▶ *sending and receiving your first email message*
▶ *disconnecting*
▶ *reading messages*

. . . .

Sending someone an email message is simple. You just need three things:

1. The person's email address.

2. An email program on your computer to send the message, such as Outlook Express or Netscape Messenger.

3. Access to an email service.

Your email address

What email addresses look like
Here are some typical examples of what email addresses look like:

admin@ukwriters.com	(a real address)
kyevalongo@internet-handbooks.co.uk	(a real address)
kyevalongo@ukwriters.com	(a real address)
jimsmith62@hotmail.com	(a fictional example)
annemariej@ukhealth.org	(a fictional example)
FilmBuffAndy@usa.net	(a fictional example)

As you can see, the address in each case is divided by the 'at' sign – @ – that you find on every typewriter and computer keyboard. This applies to all email addresses. When you speak an email address out loud, it is pronounced – taking the first example above – as 'admin at ukwriters dot com'.

▶ A correct email address is essential if your message is to reach the intended recipient.

Fast track: getting started...

The form of email addresses

As you can see, these email addresses all have rather a similar look about them. In fact, they have the standard form:

username@domain

1. The first part of an email address is called the username. This usually means the name or nickname that the person has chosen to log onto their internet service provider (ISP). This could be in an obvious and recognisable form, or the person may use some other kind of name, such as 'FilmBuffAndy'. However, most people use more or less recognisable names for their day-to-day emails.

2. @ is called the 'at' sign.

3. The last part of the address, after the @ sign, is called the 'domain' name, the name given to a specific computer on the internet. It serves a similar purpose to a house number, street name, and town name in a postal address. Some internet service providers (ISPs) use their own company name as their domain name, for example AOL, Demon, Virgin, and FreeUK. The '.com', '.org', '.net' or '.co.uk' is part of the domain. It identifies the type of organisation that the address is registered as.

Types of organisation on the internet

There are many types of organisation on the internet. The most common categories are:

.com	a commercial company or corporation
.co.uk	a UK company
.edu	an educational establishment
.gov	a government department
.net	a computer or internet services organisation
.org	an organisation, often in public service

Spaces in email addresses

Another rule to remember is that there can be no spaces in an email address. You may sometimes see email addresses with apparent gaps, but the gap will be an underline character _ (sometimes called an underscore) not a space. For example:

kye_valongo@internet-handbooks.co.uk

Your first email address

Most people using the internet from home are allocated one or more email addresses by their internet service provider. Students may be given an email address by their school, college or university. Employees are often given an email address by the organisation they work for.

Your email program

Client and server
In order to send or receive an email message, you need an email program on your computer (The technical word for this program is 'email client'.)

▶ *Client* – This usually means any computer program installed on your PC that allows you to connect to and use the services of a server. For example, your email client sends your email message to your ISP's server, which then sends it on to the recipient. Other types of client software include chat clients (for connecting to internet chat servers) and news clients (for connecting to internet news servers). A browser such as Internet Explorer or Netscape Navigator is sometimes referred to as a web client.

▶ *Server* – This is a special computer or computer program that performs some kind of service for many individual users, such as sending emails. A server that handles email for people is called a 'mail server'. Your internet service provider probably provides your mail server.

How it works
Fortunately, most modern computers come supplied with an email program ready to use. Your email program contacts your ISP's email server. This server then despatches your email message across the internet to its intended recipient.

Fig. 1. Outlook Express is perhaps the most powerful and easiest to use email client for everyday use. It also has the advantage of integrating with other Microsoft products.

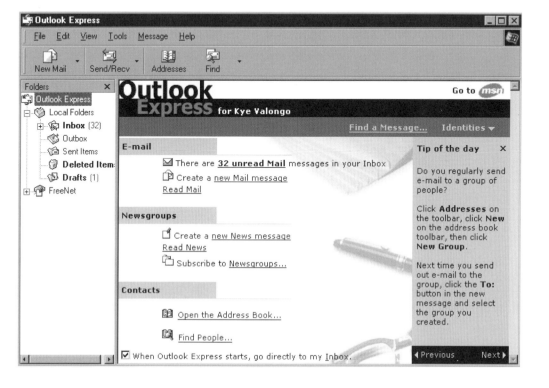

It's rather like handing an envelope to the post office. You (the client) pass the message to the counter assistant (the server) who then pops the letter into the postal system.

1. Outlook Express is the commonest and easiest email client to use. Produced by Microsoft, it looks good, and it has the advantage of working seamlessly with other Microsoft programs (such as the web browser, Internet Explorer).

2. The second most popular email program is Netscape Messenger, which comes as part of the Netscape Navigator package.

Both of these well-known email programs are well up to the job of handling your email, and have lots more useful functions besides. The vast majority of people all around the world use one or other of these programs for sending and receiving their emails.

Other email programs
Both Outlook Express and Netscape Messenger are available for free. As a result, other email clients are being pushed into the background. But two in particular – Eudora, and Pegasus Mail – are probably worth looking at, and you might even find that one of them suits you better.

If you feel like experimenting with other email clients, you do not have to get rid of Outlook Express or Netscape Messenger. You are perfectly free to use two email clients at the same time, though it could be confusing until you get used to it.

Eudora Pro, Eudora Light
http://www.eudora.com/light.html
There are three versions of Eudora: light, pay and sponsored. The light version is free but has limited options. The pay version is a powerful email client but costs money. The sponsored version is free – and as powerful as the pay version – but contains advertising. Eudora Light is old and worn around the edges because it has not been updated for a long time.

Pegasus
http://www.pegasus.usa.com/current.htm
Pegasus, like Eudora, is a favourite with many old hands on the internet. This could be either out of rebelliousness in the face of the bigger companies, or because it offers genuine value. Pegasus is particularly good if you want to run a small mailing list (see page 58).

▶ *HTML* – This refers to the special formatting commands that produce the mix of text, images and multimedia clips that comprise most web pages. Email messages with HTML content are becoming more common. Indeed, they are the default in both Outlook Express and Netscape Messenger.

Your mail server

A server that handles email for people is called a 'mail server'. Your internet service provider (ISP) probably provides your mail server, especially if you access the internet from home. An ISP is the company which provides you with a connection to the internet – just like a telephone operator can provide you with a connection to another person. Most ISPs also give you an email address – or several addresses. In addition, they enable you to send and receive email messages by letting you use their mail server.

Mail server addresses
Everyone, and every entity, connected to the internet has a specific address. For example, you have an email address, a web site has a web site address (URL or uniform resource locator), and a mail server too has an address. For example, the address of the mail server for subscribers to the UK internet service provider Virgin Net is:

mail.virgin.net

Web-based email services
If for some reason you do not have email access, or if the mail service is unacceptable to you in some way, you can easily use web-based email as described on page 76. One of the great things about the internet is that, if you can't communicate in one particular way, you can always find other ways.

Writing and reading messages

Most email clients let you compose messages much as you would write a letter in a word-processing program. For example, if you feel like it, you can change the size and format of the text, and add pictures and tables.

If you feel particularly creative, both Outlook Express and Netscape Messenger even allow you to design an email message just like a web page. This means you can add background images, hyperlinks and even sound clips and other multimedia components to your message. You can then save your designs as 'stationery' or 'templates' which you can use for future messages.

Working offline to save money
Designing and writing your email messages can sometimes take a while, especially if you have a creative impulse and don't look at the clock. Fortunately, you don't have to be connected to the internet to compose your messages. You only need to connect once you are ready to send and receive them. Sending and receiving emails normally takes only a few seconds, so you will not run up a huge phone bill just from email. Browsing the web, or spending a lot of time in chat rooms, however, will!

▶ Clicking the Send button in Outlook Express or Netscape Messenger does not necessarily connect you to the internet. It just stores your message for the time being in your Outbox or Unsent Messages Folder.

Fast track: getting started...

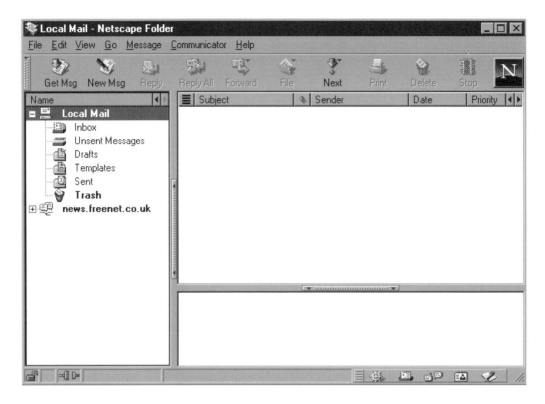

Fig. 2. Netscape Messenger is installed as standard on many computers. It comes as part of the Netscape Communicator suite of internet programs which includes Netscape Navigator and Page Composer.

Composing and sending an email message is easy

1. Open up your email program – Outlook Express or Netscape Messenger.

2. Click New Mail or New Msg.

3. Insert the email address of the intended recipient (see below for some test addresses).

4. Compose your message. This part can be as complicated or simple as you want!

For more on composing messages, see page 27.

Sending a test message
The following are some very handy test email addresses. Before you start sending messages to real people, you can practise using one or more of the addresses below, and in a few minutes an automatic reply will be sent back to you.

echo@seattlelab.com

echo@telcomplus.net

echo@tu-berlin.de

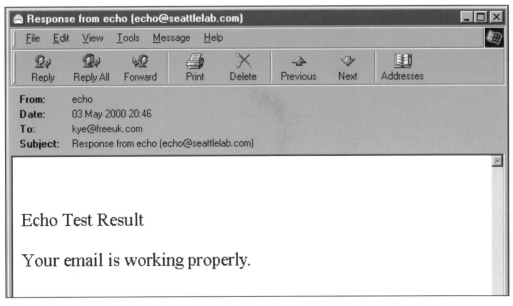

internet@gurus.com

ping@stamper.itconsult.co.uk

test-courrier@sogi.com   (in French)

test@alphanet.ch

test@mega.bw

test@netsydney.com

Fig. 3. Sending a message to one of the test addresses is the quickest way of making sure your email service is working properly. Send messages to more than one of the addresses. That way, the test will still work even if part of the internet is not working as it should.

Just send a blank message. Resist the temptation to write anything in the subject line or in body of the message, otherwise the test may fail.

Connect!

Your email client may be configured (set up) in a variety of ways. When it comes to connecting to the internet, it may try to connect and send and receive emails as soon as you start the program. This is fine, but it may not disconnect automatically afterwards – see 'Disconnecting' below.

Dial-up networking (DUN) – connecting automatically
When your email client tries to connect to the internet, it will start Windows Dial-Up Networking (Windows DUN). You will then see the Connect To window.

1. Click the Connect button. The 'Connecting to' window should now appear, as your hear your computer dialling your ISP's number.

2. Your computer will next go through the logging on sequence. During this brief process, normally a few seconds, your username and pass-word are each verified.

17

Fast track: getting started..

Fig. 4. Windows dial-up networking, the Connect To box. It shows Molly's computer dialling up to her ISP, a company called Madasafish. The box shows the ISP's telephone number (0845 3504005). Molly has clicked 'Save password' to save herself having to type it in next time she dials up.

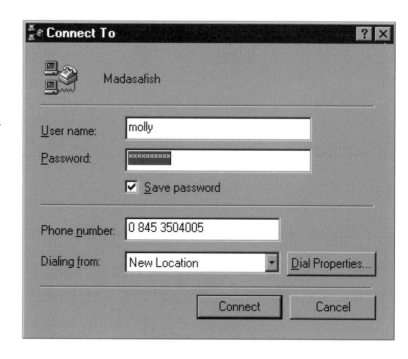

Fig. 5. Windows dial-up networking: the window icon is now minimised, and sits on the bottom edge of your screen. You can restore it at any time by clicking on it.

Fig. 6. Windows dial-up networking: connected. The connexion box shows the connexion speed, in this case 115,200 bits per second. It also shows the time so far spent online (18 seconds), and the amount of data sent and received, measured in bytes.

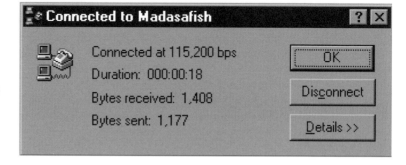

3. Once you are connected, the 'Connecting to' notice will disappear. DUN minimises to a small icon on your Start menu, as in figure 5. (If you double-click this icon it will reappear as in figure 6. You can minimise it again at any time if you wish.)

Connecting manually
If for some reason, your email client does not start DUN, you will have to connect manually. This is how to do it step-by-step:

1. On your Desktop, double-click My Computer.

2. In the Dial-Up Networking window, click the connection for your ISP.

3. Enter your username and password.

4. Click Connect.

Sending and receiving your first email messages

Once you are connected, start your email client (normally Outlook Express or Netscape Messenger). This will tell it to immediately despatch any mail sitting in your Outbox. It will also collect any incoming email waiting for you at the mail server.

Both Outlook Express and Netscape Messenger will send and retrieve your email messages automatically, when set up correctly. In fact, you can also set them up to check for new emails periodically while you are online doing other things, say browsing the web.

If your email client is already running, or has not tried to collect messages, do the following to send and retrieve messages:

1. In Outlook Express, click the Send/Recv button.

2. In Netscape Messenger, click the Get Msg button.

Any incoming messages will appear in your Inbox.

Disconnecting

To save on your telephone bill, disconnect from the internet once all your new incoming messages have been retrieved. You can read them at leisure when you are not connected, in other words when you are offline.

To disconnect, double-click the small DUN icon on your Windows toolbar. When it has enlarged ('restored') on your screen, click on its Disconnect button. You can also right-click on the icon and select Disconnect in the pop-up menu.

Reading messages

To read a message, simply find it in your Inbox then double-click on it. Single-clicking will also work. However, if you do this you will see the contents of the message in the preview pane or your email client, instead of in a separate window.

How to find your Inbox folder in Outlook Express:

1. Open the View menu.

2. Click Go to Folder

3. Select Inbox.

4. Click OK.

Fig. 7. If you ever get
lost, go to the View menu
on the main toolbar. Here
you can control the
appearance of Netscape
Messenger, either to
customise it, or to get it
back to the way it was
before.

How to find your Inbox folder in Netscape Messenger:

(a) Open the View menu.

(b) Click Show.

(c) Click Folders, so that a tick appears beside it.

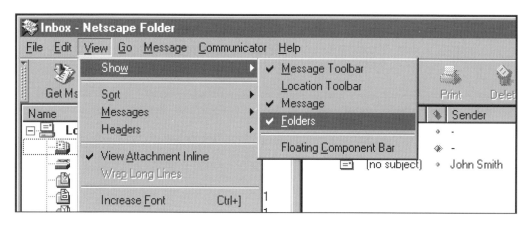

2 Sending and replying to emails

In this chapter we will explore:

▶ *finding someone's email address*
▶ *your email address book*
▶ *replying to a message*
▶ *forwarding a message*
▶ *sending an email to more than one person*
▶ *formatting your message text*
▶ *adding graphics to your messages*
▶ *adding a sound track to your messages*
▶ *more HTML tips*
▶ *when not to use HTML for email messages*

. . . .

Finding someone's email address

Unlike with telephone numbers, there is no one company or organisation that deals with email addresses. Consequently, there are no real equivalents of national telephone directories. Instead the email directories on the web rely on people registering their own email address in some way. The problem is that many people don't bother registering. This is in part because they don't know about the service, and in part because they see the sense of keeping their email address private.

Some of the directories also harvest email addresses from other parts of the internet such as Usenet postings and people's web sites. Even so, many of the entries become out of date. However, you might find it worthwhile exploring one of the better email directories. Here are two of them:

Bigfoot
http://uk.bigfoot.com
All you need to do is enter the person's first and last name and click the Search button. You will then be given a list of email addresses for people in the directory with that name.

Yahoo People Search
http://people.yahoo.com/
This is another excellent site, run by the world's most popular search engine and internet directory.

Try it with my name. Type in Bigfoot's address into your browser's address box, remembering to hit the Return key on your keyboard. When the Bigfoot page is displayed in your browser window, find the search box and type in 'Kye Valongo'. Bigfoot will then show you several email addresses that I have used in the past, and possibly one or two for other 'Kye Valongos' (there are not many of us!). If you try with a name like

Sending and replying to emails ....

Address   http://people.yahoo.com/   ▼   Lin

YAHOO! PEOPLE SEARCH   Yahoo! - Email - Address

Yahoo! Messenger - online friends, instant messaging, voice chat

Welcome, Guest User   Create My Listi

Yahoo! People Search   FIND   Search

Merchant Spotlight   **Telephone Search**

FREE CALLS
deltathree.com
Great Calling
Rates Worldwide!

First Name   **Last Name**(required)

City/Town   **State**   Search   Reset

Yahoo! Resources
· Yellow Pages   **Email Search**

Fig. 8. Yahoo! and Bigfoot are the biggest email directories and your best means of finding someone's address – apart from asking them personally, of course.

John Smith you will be overwhelmed by thousands of addresses. Pin-pointing the one you need will take more time.

If the person has a common name like Smith, you will have to either search through thousands of Smiths or use an advanced search. On both the Bigfoot and the Yahoo! sites, you can perform an advanced directory search. This means that you can additionally search for the town where that person lives, or the organisation that he or she works for, or the node. For example, if you know that John Smith lives in Crewe and has an email address ending with 'freeserve.com', you can narrow down the list that the directory gives you.

▶ *A node* – is the part of an email address that comes after the @ sign. For example, in the email address kye@freeuk.com, the node is free-uk.com.

Unfortunately, the reality is that the entries in email directories are often out of date and the addresses difficult to find. If you have some other way of contacting the person, it would be far simpler just to ask them for their email address.

Your email address book

Email addresses are often very awkward-looking and difficult to remember. But, just as you would keep the addresses of your friends and colleagues in an address book, so you can store the email addresses of your internet contacts in a special electronic address book. This handy item is part of your email client, such as Outlook Express or Netscape

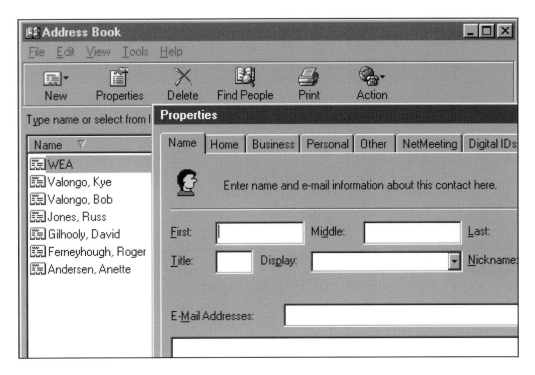

Messenger. Your address book will store not only email addresses but also many other useful details such as name, address, phone numbers, website address, fax number and job description.

▶ Netscape Messenger has its own address book, based on the principle of a card index.

▶ Outlook Express shares the Windows address book that usually comes installed on all Windows PCs.

Fig. 9. The Outlook Express address book allows you to record much more than just a person's email address. You can also record their street address, telephone number and more.

Outlook Express
To add an entry to the address book in Outlook Express:

1. Open the Tools menu.
2. Select Address Book.
3. Open the File menu.
4. Select New Contact.
5. Type in the details you want to store in the address book including the email address.

Netscape Messenger
To add an entry in Netscape Messenger's address book:

(a) Open the File menu.

(b) Select New Card.

Sending and replying to emails ....

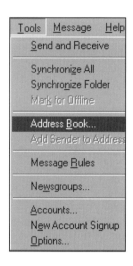

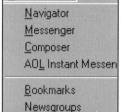

(c) Fill in the details.

Sending an email message using the address book
Once you have stored someone's email address in the address book, you will be able to send that person a message with a couple of mouse clicks instead of having to type in their email address by hand. All you need to do is open the address book, find the person's entry and click on the command for a new message.

In Outlook Express

1. Open the Tools menu.

2. Select Address Book.

3. Right-click your mouse over the person's entry.

4. Select Action, then Send Mail.

In Netscape Messenger

(a) Open the Communicator menu.

(b) Select Address Book.

(c) Right-click your mouse over the person's entry.

(d) Select New Message.

Replying to a message

To reply to a message is even easier than using the address book. Just open the message and click on the Reply button. When you reply to a message, your email client will automatically fill in the email address. It will also include the content of the original message in the body of the reply. This is usual with internet messages because otherwise it can become confusing and difficult to remember what was written in which email.

For example, if you email a friend and ask 'What is your daughter's favourite colour?' it may be a few days before the friend has time to reply. Then, unexpectedly, you receive an email with the word 'blue' in the message and little else. If you have an inbox full of messages, it may take you a while to work out what the 'blue' refers to. However, if each message quoted the original messages, for example:

> >What is your daughter's favourite colour?
> Blue

Then there would be no doubt. The > character, or something similar, is the usual way to indicate a line quoted from the received message. There will be times when replies become more complicated, and quoted quotes make an appearance. Take for example the following two further replies:

> > >What is your daughter's favourite colour?
> > Blue

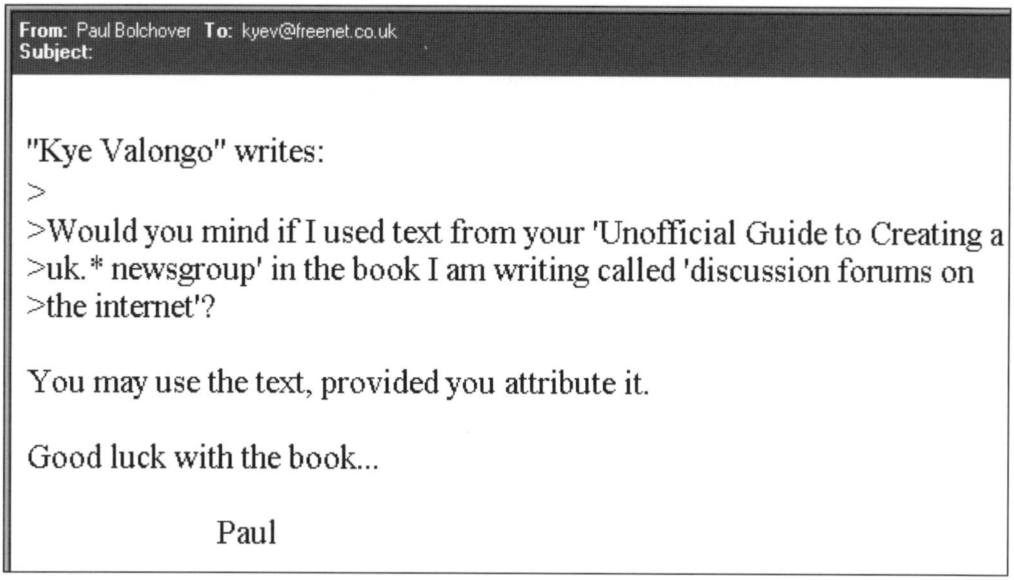

From: Paul Bolchover To: kyev@freenet.co.uk
Subject:

"Kye Valongo" writes:
>
>Would you mind if I used text from your 'Unofficial Guide to Creating a
>uk.* newsgroup' in the book I am writing called 'discussion forums on
>the internet'?

You may use the text, provided you attribute it.

Good luck with the book...

      Paul

What shade?

To which the reply could be:

>>> What is your daughter's favourite colour?
>> Blue
> What shade?
Manchester City blue!

Fig. 10. Some email replies can become very confusing with quotes or quoted quotes running down the page. Before you reply, try where possible to cut out ('snip') the parts of a message that are no longer relevant.

Note the multiple use of > by the email clients.

Obviously, you don't have to include all the various quotes every time, especially if the dialogue becomes long and complicated – you can just quote the relevant parts and 'snip' (cut out) the rest to save space.

Forwarding a message

Forwarding a message is almost identical to replying to one, except that you address it to a person other than the one who sent it. You might for example want to forward a joke you have received, to another of your friends.

When you reply to a message, your email client automatically fills in the email address of the person who sent it. When you forward a message, you must supply the email address of the recipient yourself, either by using your address book or by typing it in yourself.

To forward a message

1. Select the message you want to forward.

2. Click the Forward button (in either Outlook Express and Netscape Messenger).

Sending and replying to emails ....

3. Fill in the address of the recipient. Use your address book if appropriate.

4. Add your comments.

5. Click Send.

The contents of the original message are included in the message similar to when you reply to someone. You can also, of course, add your own message or comments to the message.

Sending an email to more than one person

When you send an email message to someone, you put their email address in the 'To:' section. If you want to send the same message to other people, you do not have to write everything out again. You just include their addresses in the 'Cc:' section. 'Cc:' stands for carbon copy. The term is derived from the traditional office environment where sending copies of business letters to other interested parties is usual practice. The other recipients are listed at the bottom of the letter in a 'Cc:' list.

▶ *Example* – 'Cc:' would be useful if you wanted to notify several different people of an event. You could send a wedding invitation to all of your friends and family by writing just one message. You would address it to one person, and put the addresses of all of the other people in the 'Cc:' section; everyone will receive the same message. Also, everyone will be able to see who else has been invited.

What if there is someone whose email address you do not want to appear in the list? After all, not all guests at a wedding will be popular with one another. Suppose there is someone you want to invite, but you know that if the others hear about it, they would not come themselves. You can hide that person's address by putting it in the 'Bcc:' section. 'Bcc:' stands for blind carbon copy. Any email addresses in the 'Bcc:' section will be invisible to other recipients of the message. Simple!

Outlook Express
To enter an address in the 'Bcc:' section of Outlook Express:

1. Start a new message.

2. Fill in the addresses of the other intended recipients of the message in the 'To:' and 'Cc:' sections. Use your address book if appropriate.

3. Open the View menu.

4. Select View All Headers to show the 'Bcc:' section.

5. Fill in the address of the invisible recipient. Use your address book if appropriate.

Netscape Messenger
To enter addresses in the 'Cc:' and 'Bcc:' section in Netscape Messenger:

(a) Start a new message.

(b) Fill in the address of the recipient of the message in the 'To:' section. Use your address book if appropriate.

(c) Press enter.

(d) Click the 'To:' button on the next line and select 'Cc:'

(e) Enter the other recipients' addresses separated by semicolons if there are more than one. Use your address book if appropriate.

(f) Click the 'To:' button on the next line and select 'Bcc:'

(g) Enter the invisible recipients' addresses separated by semicolons if there are more than one.

(h) Once you have filled in the addresses, compose your message as normal, and click Send.

Formatting your message text

In the early days, email messages were always text only. They were all one type size, and there were no special effects like bold, italics or underlined text. Now, however, email clients have the same kind of power as a good word-processing program. As a result, you can change the appearance of your messages in many ways.

Fig. 11. The Outlook Express stationery wizard helps you to format your emails in a variety of colourful ways. You can use in-built designs or create your own from your favourite colours and images.

Stationery Setup Wizard   ☒

Welcome to the stationery wizard.

Stationery is a template for composing HTML messages. You can include a background picture and position, background color, customize the font, and set the margins.

< Back | Next > | Cancel

27

Sending and replying to emails ....

Formatting the text in HTML
Email messages are formatted with hypertext markup language (HTML), the same standard as used for formatting web pages. With HTML, you can use many different kinds of fonts, text sizes, and colours.

Outlook Express
The first step is to start a new email message. Then make sure that HTML formatting is turned on by opening the Format menu. If the black dot appears by Rich Text (HTML), it means that HTML formatting is turned on. To HTML-format all outgoing messages with Outlook Express:

1. Open the Tools menu.

2. Click Options, and then the Send tab.

3. In the Mail Sending Format, click HTML.

You can change the way all your messages look or you can make changes to selected text within a message.

To change the text style for all messages
In the Tools menu, click Options. Next, click the Compose tab, and then the Font Settings button.

To format text within individual messages
Select the text you want to change. Then use the formatting toolbar to create the effect you want.

Netscape Messenger
In Netscape Messenger, to use HTML in your messages:

1. Open the Edit menu.

2. Select Preferences.

3. Click on the Formatting part of the Mail and Newsgroups section.

4. Click on 'Use HTML editor to compose messages'.

When you start a new message thereafter, you will be able to format it using HTML. Select the text you want, and use the Format menu to change the appearance of your text.

Adding graphics to your messages

Using HTML formatting also enables you to add graphics to your messages.

Outlook Express
To insert a picture in Outlook Express:

1. Click the exact point in your message where you want the image to appear.

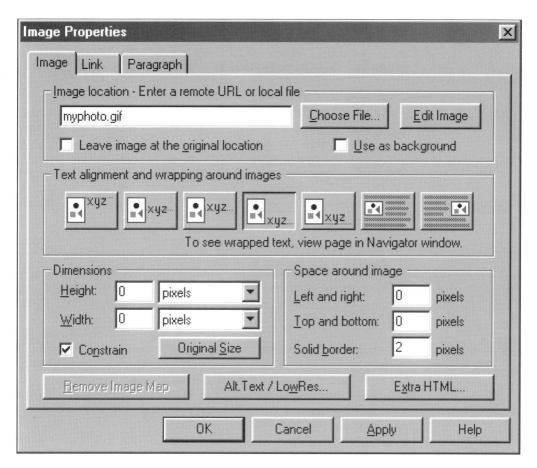

2. Open the Insert menu, and click Picture. Then click Browse to find your image file on your computer.

3. Change the layout and spacing of the image.

If the Picture command is not available, turn on HTML formatting. You do this by opening the Format menu and then clicking RichText (HTML). A black dot should be visible next to the command.

To set a picture to be used as a background for a message, click the Format menu. Next, select Background, then Picture. Click the Browse button to search your computer for the image you want to use.

Netscape Messenger
In Netscape Messenger, too, you can easily insert a picture anywhere into your email message. Open your message composition window. Then, on the mail Messenger toolbar, click Insert, then Image.

Adding a sound track to your messages

Outlook Express
Outlook Express makes it easy to include a sound in a message. Then, as

Fig. 12. Inserting an image into an email using Netscape Messenger. Here, the sender has selected a file called 'myphoto.gif' and chosen to put a 2-pixel solid border around it.

soon as someone views your message, it will play the sound. To insert a sound with your message:

1. Click anywhere in the Message window.

2. Open the Format menu. Click Background, then Sound.

3. Enter the name of the sound file you want to include, and the number of times you want the file to play.

Netscape Messenger
Unfortunately, Netscape Messenger has no obvious way of using sound within an email message. The final version of Netscape 6 due out soon may change this.

More HTML tips

If you know how to design even a simple web page, then you will be able to apply that skill to designing an email message or template. You may have designed, or have in mind, a particular web page for the purpose. You can tweak any other features that need to be tweaked.

There are a couple of disadvantages to sending fancy email messages that have been designed in this way. First, if you use somebody else's web page design without changing it out of recognition, you may be liable for some kind of copyright violation. Second, the size of the message may increase so much that it takes a long time for you to send it. By the same token, the recipient will have to spend more time downloading the message – thus increasing his or her telephone bill.

Outlook Express
However, if you still want to try this, open Outlook Express. Then:

1. Open the Message menu.

2. Choose 'New Message Using'

3. Select Web Page.

4. Enter the URL or location of the web page you want to use.

To use a page on the web, enter the URL of the page, for example:

http://www.ukwriters.com/index.htm

To use a page that is stored on your computer, enter the location. It will be something like this:

C:\My Documents\mywebpage.htm

Netscape Messenger
There is no easy way to use Netscape Messenger in the same way.

When not to use HTML for email messages

When you use HTML formatting in an email message, you may find that some email clients cannot read HTML. Consequently, a recipient may be unable to read your message. The message may be totally unreadable or appear as plain text with an HTML file attached.

No problem, though. You can set up your client so that your messages are sent in a readable format.

In Outlook Express

1. Open theTools menu.

2. Choose Options.

3. Click the Send tab.

4. Click on the Reply to messages using the format in which they were sent check box so that a cross appears in the box.

In Netscape Messenger

(a) Open the Edit menu.

(b) Choose Preferences.

(c) In the Mail and Newsgroups section, click the Formatting section.

(d) In the section entitled 'When sending HTML messages to recipients who are not listed as being able to receive them', click 'Convert the message into plain text.'

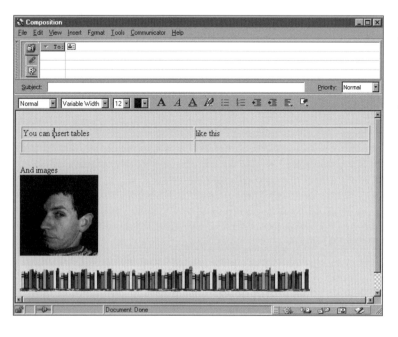

Fig. 13. The HTML formatting capabilities of Netscape Messenger are more limited than Outlook Express but there is still an amazing amount that you can do.

Sending and replying to emails......................................

There are few email clients today that cannot read HTML messages. However, many people don't like to receive messages unless they are in plain text. You can opt to send all your messages in plain text to make things simple – but with the increasing speeds of internet connection and the availability of so many wonderful designs, why not add a little colour?

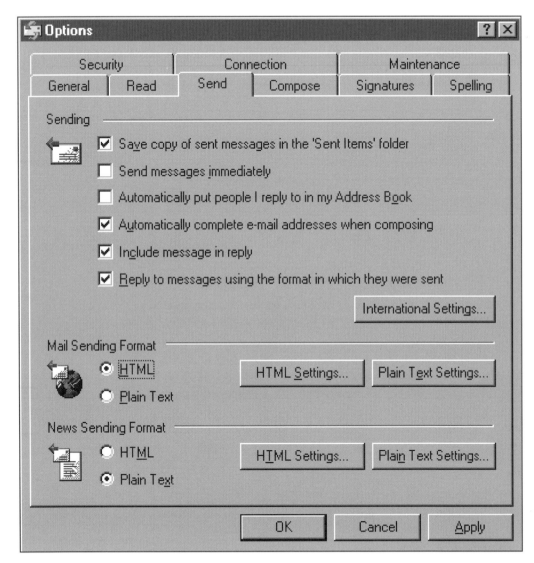

Fig. 14. Messages formatted with HTML may not be readable by everyone. Also, they may take a long time to send and receive. Don't upset someone with a large message that they can't read. Check with them first.

3 Managing your emails

In this chapter we will explore:

▶ *sorting messages*
▶ *deleting messages*
▶ *organising your messages into folders*
▶ *filtering your incoming emails*
▶ *filtering emails in Outlook Express*
▶ *filtering emails in Netscape Messenger*
▶ *junk email*
▶ *defending yourself against spam*
▶ *identifying the sender of an email*
▶ *where to complain*
▶ *how to view message headers*
▶ *don't be a spammer*

. . . .

After a while, email messages will start to accumulate in your inbox. Most email clients will allow you to manage your email in a variety of ways both manually and automatically. You can sort, delete, copy, move, and filter messages in many different ways.

Sorting messages

The messages that you have received are displayed in a number of columns, for example:

Subject

Sender

Date

You can sort the display in any of these columns by clicking the column title. For example, to order the messages alphabetically by sender (A–Z), click the title Sender at the top of the column. A second click will put them in reverse order (Z–A). Ordering the messages by date is perhaps the most useful because then the newest messages appear at the top, or at the bottom if you click twice.

Deleting messages

When you have begun to amass a number of incoming messages, you may want to tidy up your Inbox. Deleting messages is the easiest way. It's just a click away. First, select (highlight) the messages you want to delete. Then, in Outlook Express click the Delete button, or in Netscape Messenger click Delete Message.

After you delete a message, however, it is not lost. It is transferred from

Managing your emails ....

your Inbox folder to another folder, the:

▶ Deleted Items folder in Outlook Express. Note: Outlook Express may automatically empty the Deleted Items folder each time you exit.

▶ Trash folder in Netscape Messenger. Note: the deleted messages remain there until you instruct Messenger to delete them permanently.

However, Sent mail also remains in the Sent Mail folder until it is deleted, so look in there if you want to free up some space.

Highlight message and click the Delete button

Fig. 15. Deleting an unwanted email message in Outlook Express.

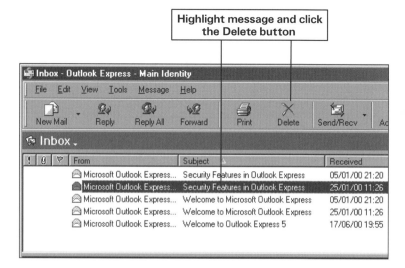

Highlight message and click the Delete button

Fig. 16. Deleting an unwanted email message in Netscape Messenger.

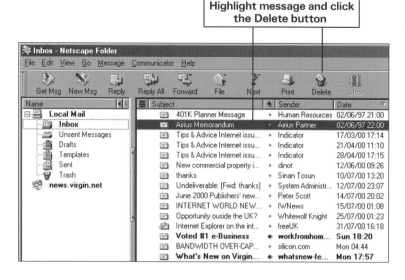

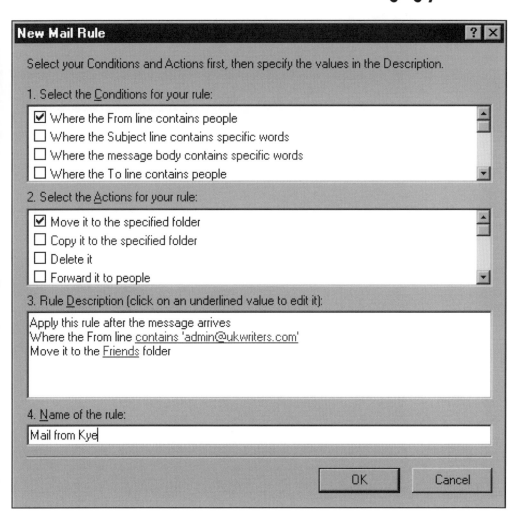

New Mail Rule   ? ☒

Select your Conditions and Actions first, then specify the values in the Description.

1. Select the Conditions for your rule:

☑ Where the From line contains people
☐ Where the Subject line contains specific words
☐ Where the message body contains specific words
☐ Where the To line contains people

2. Select the Actions for your rule:

☑ Move it to the specified folder
☐ Copy it to the specified folder
☐ Delete it
☐ Forward it to people

3. Rule Description (click on an underlined value to edit it):

Apply this rule after the message arrives
Where the From line contains 'admin@ukwriters.com'
Move it to the Friends folder

4. Name of the rule:

Mail from Kye

                                    OK   Cancel

Organising your messages into folders

As well as deleting messages, you can use your email client to create new folders, and move messages into those folders according to the type of messages they are. If you send and receive a lot of emails, then organising them all into folders will make life easier. For example, you might want one folder specifically for your family and friends, another for regular news-letters, and another for your business emails.

Outlook Express
To create a new folder in Outlook Express:

1. Select your inbox in the folders pane.

2. Click on File, then New, and select New Folder.

3. Give the new folder a name, such as 'Mum and dad'.

Fig. 17. You can create filters to move mail from known sources – friends, mailing lists, and so on – to various separate folders. Anything else that appears in your in-tray will be immediately identifiable as coming from an unknown source.

Managing your emails ....

Fig. 18. Creating a new folder in Outlook Express, called 'Mum and dad'.

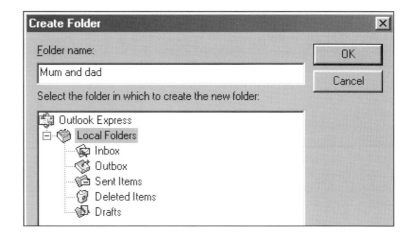

Fig. 19. Creating a new folder in Netscape Messenger, called 'Uncle Fred'.

Netscape Messenger
To create a new folder in Netscape Messenger:

(a) Click on the File menu, then New Folder.

(b) Give the new folder a name.

(c) Select which existing folder the new one should be created in.

(d) Click OK.

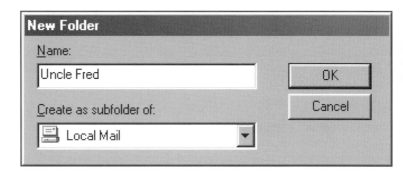

Now you can move or copy messages from your inbox into the new folder by clicking and dragging.

Filtering your incoming emails

Most newsreaders allow the use of filters. The criteria you decide to use to filter messages can be any part of the incoming messages or articles:

Who the message is to.

Who it is from.

What the subject contains.

What the body text contains.

Your client can scan incoming emails and move them to different directories according to who they are from. Your client can also perform many
other tasks automatically when you connect: it will copy, delete, reply,
forward, mark, and so on.

Some email clients and newsreaders enable you to set multiple filters
to look at different parts of a message. They can carry out various tasks
depending on what the filters find. For example, if you receive a message
from a mailing list (see page 58), you could have the email program
automatically move it to a special folder. If it comes from a named
person on that list, it could mark it in colour to make you aware of it.

Filtering emails in Outlook Express

When you have lots of incoming email, Outlook Express can help you
process it more efficiently. For example, you can use 'rules' to automatically sort it into different folders and reply to or forward certain messages.

Creating a rule for mail messages
1. On the Tools menu, click on Message Rules, then Mail.

2. On the Mail Rules tab, click New.

3. Select the conditions for your rule by ticking at least one of the check
    boxes in Conditions.

4. You can specify multiple conditions for a single rule by ticking more
    than one check box.

5. Select the actions for your rule by ticking at least one of the check
    boxes in the Actions section.

6. Click the underlined hyperlinks in Rule Description, to specify the
    conditions or actions for your rule.

7. In the Rule Description section you can click Contains People, or Con-
    tains Specific Words, to specify the people or words you want Out-
    look Express to look out for in messages. If you enter multiple
    people or multiple words per condition, use the Options button in
    the Select People or Type Specific Words dialog boxes to further cus-
    tomise the condition.

8. In the Name of the rule box, select the default name. Then type a new
    name for your rule, and click OK.

Managing your emails ....

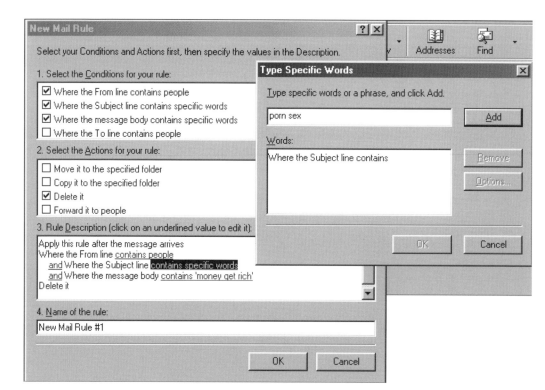

New Mail Rule

Select your Conditions and Actions first, then specify the values in the Description.

1. Select the Conditions for your rule:

☑ Where the From line contains people
☑ Where the Subject line contains specific words
☑ Where the message body contains specific words
☐ Where the To line contains people

2. Select the Actions for your rule:

☐ Move it to the specified folder
☐ Copy it to the specified folder
☑ Delete it
☐ Forward it to people

3. Rule Description (click on an underlined value to edit it):

Apply this rule after the message arrives
Where the From line contains people
   and Where the Subject line contains specific words
   and Where the message body contains 'money get rich'
Delete it

4. Name of the rule:

New Mail Rule #1

OK   Cancel

Type Specific Words

Type specific words or a phrase, and click Add.

porn sex   Add

Words:

Where the Subject line contains   Remove
                                         Options...

OK   Cancel

Addresses   Find

Fig. 20. Setting up filtering rules in Outlook Express to delete unwanted incoming messages.

Changing a rule

1. On the Tools menu, click Message Rules, then Mail.

2. Choose the rule you want to change, and click Modify.

3. Make your changes in the Edit Rule dialog box. Remember to rename the rule. Then click OK.

Applying a rule to messages already received

Any new rules you create will apply to new incoming messages. This is how to apply rules to messages you have already received:

1. On the Tools menu, click on Message Rules, then Mail.

2. In the Message Rules dialog box, click Apply Now.

3. Select the rules you want to apply to messages already downloaded. Click Select All if you want to apply all your current rules.

4. Click the Browse button to choose the folders you want to apply the selected rules to.

5. Click Apply Now to apply the selected rules to the folders you have chosen.

▶ *Finding out more* – On the main toolbar of Outlook Express, click Help then Contents and Index.

Filtering emails in Netscape Messenger

You can set up and use message filters so that Messenger automatically matches your filtering criteria. This can include filing messages in a special folder as soon as they arrive. To create a filter to sift through incoming messages:

1. In the Messenger window, click on Edit, then Message Filters.

2. In the Message Filters dialog box, click New. You will then see the Filter Rules dialog box. Here you enter whatever information is needed to define your filter.

To edit a filter
You can use the Message Filters Rules dialog box to edit or define an action of your filters. You can also specify the type of messages you want to be filtered.

1. Type a name for your filter.

2. Select the Match option you want. Use the pop-up menus to choose filtering criteria. Then, type a keyword to be used in the search.

3. If you want to add some new filtering criteria, click More. If you want to remove some, click Fewer. Then use the filtering action you want.

Fig. 21. Setting up filtering rules in Netscape Messenger.

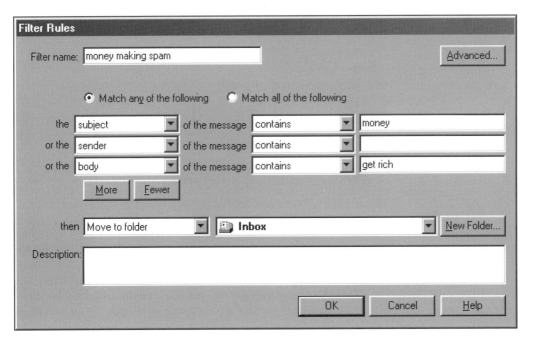

4. Click New Folder to create a new mail folder.

5. Type some descriptive information about this filter in the Description field.

6. If you want to enter customised header information, click Advanced.

To delete a filter
Select the filter name and click Delete.

To switch a filter on or off
To turn a filter on, click the dot to the right of the filter name (checkmark). To turn it off, click the checkmark (dot).

To change the filtering sequence
In the filter list, click a filter's name. Then click the up or down arrow to move it to a different part of the sequence.

To log filter activity
Logging filter activity can help to debug filtering. Click the checkbox at Log Filter Use. When you want to display the filter log, click View Log.

Junk email
Spam and Unsolicited Commercial Email (UCE) are terms that refer to junk mail. It may be sent to you personally by email or posted across many Usenet newsgroups – sometimes hundreds. The term spam comes from the use of the word in a Monty Python sketch, where the word was repeated over and over again. On the internet, it has come to refer to the practice of sending out hundreds or thousands of unwanted messages.

The email version of spam usually has an absurd title that gives it away, such as:

'!!!! How I made five thousand pounds in a single day !!!!'

All spam is unwanted, and most of it is probably also illegal.

If you are new to the internet your mailbox will be fairly quiet. But, rest assured, once you have been around for a while, the professional information harvesters and data gatherers will have obtained your details, and you will be seen as fair game.

Defending yourself against spam

Some people who spam don't know when to stop. Sooner or later you may have to do something to stem the tide of junk arriving in your inbox. The best way is to hit the spammers in their Achilles heel – their own internet service provider. ISPs often have very strict policies prohibiting the sending of unsolicited email. They will tend to act swiftly – for example, by imposing fines, issuing warnings, or cutting off the offender's access to the internet. The ISP's reaction will be more severe if the offending 'marketers' have forged their own email address, or if their messages contain verbal abuse.

```
Subj:        I Need 49 People            kosemi
Date:        12/10/00 08:11:26 GMT Daylight Time
From:        jadasom@ihojula.com
Reply-to:    jadasom@ihojula.com
To:          jdrbwilliams28@aol.com


Hello Friend,

I would like to welcome you to your future.
    Would You LIke:
* Personal Freedom
* Unlimited Income
* Peace Of Mind
* Limitless Opportunities
* More Free Time With Your Family

CLICK HERE NOW TO CHANGE YOUR LIFE FOR THE BETTER

P.S . I will Take ONLY 49 people And Teach them the way to make
money on the Net.
```

1. Always confirm that the email is unsolicited.

2. Identify the real sender if possible, and their ISP.

3. Send off your complaint to the ISP concerned.

Solicited or unsolicited?
Is the email unsolicited? Before you put on your war paint, check whether the message has come from some mailing list or other that you signed up to while browsing the web, maybe weeks or months ago. You may have forgotten that you signed up. Or perhaps you did not associate it with the annoying email you have received. Again, some other person might have used your computer to sign up to the mailing list.

If it is a mailing list, the answer is to unsubscribe (see page 64). There is a proper way of doing this if you no longer want to receive the messages. Most mailing lists include instructions with each message on how to unsubscribe.

▶ *Tip* – If you do decide to send a complaint, be polite, or at least civil. The person receiving your complaint will not usually be the one responsible for the spam, and may hate spam every bit as much as you.

Spammers usually forge the return addresses in their junk messages but sometimes you can identify the true sender.

Fig. 22. Spam or unsolicited mail is worse than the junk you receive through your letterbox, because you have to pay (your phone bill) for receiving it.

Identifying the sender of an email

Look in the header of the message to see if there is an address where you should send complaints. Some ISPs include special lines in the header, such as those for NetscapeOnline and Freeserve respectively:

X-Report: Report abuse to abuse@netscapeonline.co.uk

X-Complaints-To: abuse@theplanet.net

If there is an abuse header, send your complaint there; if not, you may have to do some guesswork. Look at the sender's email address, e.g. molly@madasafish.com. You can be sure, in the majority of cases, that the ISP is identifiable from what comes after the @ sign (in this case, Madasafish). Some other well-known examples are included in the table below.

Email address	ISP	Abuse address
someone@aol.com	AOL	abuse@aol.com
someone@breathemail.net	Breathemail	abuse@vip.uk.com
someone@btinternet.com	BT	abuse@btinternet.com
someone@somewhere.demon.co.uk	Demon	abuse@demon.net
someone@free4all.co.uk	Free4all	abuse@in2home.net
someone@somewhere.freeserve.co.uk	Freeserve	abuse@theplanet.net
someone@tesco.net	Tesco	abuse@uk.uu.net
someone@ukonline.co.uk	UKonline	abuse@ukonline.net

As you can see, the names of most of the ISPs can be worked out simply by looking at the sender's email address.

Where to complain

Once you know which ISP is involved, send them a copy of your complaint. Be sure to attach a copy of the junk mail, including all of the headers, and send it to the abuse address. If it is not clear where you should send your complaint, send copies to various addresses at their ISP. For instance, you should always send a copy to:

postmaster@site (e.g. postmaster@demon.net)

The Postmaster is traditionally the person who deals with problems or abuses. However, quite a number of sites don't have a postmaster address. So you should also send a copy to:

admin@site

and, to be absolutely certain, send it to:

root@site

How to view message headers

Outlook Express
To view all of the headers, in Outlook Express, right-click on the message, select Properties, then the Details tab, and click the Message Source button. Now copy and paste the full message into your complaint.

Netscape Messenger
If you use Netscape Messenger, select the View menu. Select Headers, then All.

Incorrect email addresses
As mentioned, some of the above email addresses may not be correct. For example, a given ISP may not have set up an abuse account. In this case the email will be returned to you with an error message advising that there was no such user. But at least one of your email messages will find its way to the complaints department.

Often, you get a message sent by an autoresponder. This will be a brief message confirming that your email has been received. The message will normally tell you what steps are being taken to investigate your complaint or details of who to send future complaints to.

A great list of abuse addresses is held here:

http://www.abuse.net/cgi-bin/list-abuse-addresses

If you have identified the sender's ISP, you can take a look at:

Abuse.net
http://www.abuse.net/
They say: 'The Abuse.net system helps forward messages about abusive activity on the internet to people who can do something about it.'

Managing your emails ....

NETWORK **ABUSE**
CLEARINGHOUSE

Welcome to the Network Abuse Clearinghouse

Updated March 3, 2000

The Network Abuse Clearinghouse is intended to help the Internet community to report and control network abuse and abusive users.

Since the best place to report abusive activity varies from one system to another, we're trying to keep a master database of reporting addresses for users throughout the net to use. The database is provided in three forms:

- Via a mail forwarding service
- Via a web look-up page
- Via a WHOIS server at whois.abuse.net

For e-mail users

You can use abuse.net to help forward your complaints to system managers who can act on them. Please read

Fig. 23. Unwanted email is like acne. If you don't take early action, you could soon be overwhelmed. Network Abuse Clearinghouse can help you.

Abuse.net forwards messages from you to the most effective complaint handler at the ISP.

Your own ISP
If all fails, contact your own ISP support staff. They will be able to help you because it is in their own interest to prevent spam from tying up their mail servers and irritating their own customers.

Don't be a spammer

You may think that sending thousands of email messages is a good way of making a lot of money. Don't even think of it. Spam is a complete waste of time both for the recipient and for the sender of the spam. You may think that, once your message gets sent to millions of people, you will reap vast rewards for a minimum outlay.

The reality is far less attractive. A few minutes after your 'campaign' has started your inbox will explode with abusive messages, mail bombs (huge files designed to overload your system), and viruses. The replies from genuine potential customers will be lost in the mayhem. A few days later, your ISP will shut down your account, or take you to court. Your name and website may even be placed on blacklists kept by many organisations, including ISPs. You will be blacklisted as an internet user for a very long time.

4 Sending and receiving files

In this chapter we will explore:

▶ *attaching files to emails*
▶ *compressing files*
▶ *compression software*
▶ *decompressing files*
▶ *breaking up large messages*
▶ *the threat of viruses*
▶ *protecting against virus infection*
▶ *antivirus software*

. . . .

Attaching files to emails

There is much more to email than just sending text messages. You can send all kinds of other computer files as 'attachments' to your email messages. For example, you can attach:

1. word-processed documents
2. spreadsheets
3. pictures
4. animations
5. video clips
6. sound tracks
7. software programs
8. databases

You may want to send copies of your wedding photos to a relative in another country or a spreadsheet to a work colleague. You can send just one file, or a whole number of files, attached to one email message.

Attaching a file to an email
This is how to attach a file to your outgoing email message:

1. Start a new message.

2. Open Windows Explorer and find ('browse for') the file you wish to send.

3. Drag and drop the file onto the new message.

Using Outlook Express
If you use Outlook Express, just drag and drop the file you want to attach, onto the message body.

Using Netscape Messenger
If you use Netscape Messenger, drag and drop the file you want to attach onto the subject line, or the addressing area of the message.

Sending and receiving files ....

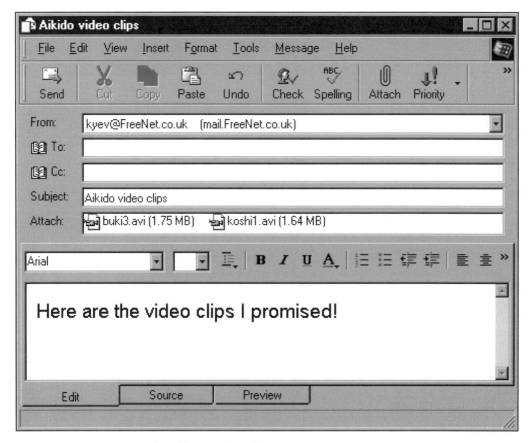

Aikido video clips

| File | Edit | View | Insert | Format | Tools | Message | Help |

Send | Cut | Copy | Paste | Undo | Check | Spelling | Attach | Priority

From: kyev@FreeNet.co.uk (mail.FreeNet.co.uk)

To:

Cc:

Subject: Aikido video clips

Attach: buki3.avi (1.75 MB)   koshi1.avi (1.64 MB)

Arial   B I U A

Here are the video clips I promised!

Edit   Source   Preview

Fig. 24. Outlook Express handles attachments efficiently. Double-click, and you can save the file to disk. Be extremely careful before you run any software program that is attached to a message. Check it for viruses first.

Attaching very large files

Some files can be very large, well over one megabyte for example (1,000 kilobytes). These will accordingly take a long time to send, thereby increasing telephone costs both for you and your intended recipient. Scanned images, for example, can often be very large. Depending on their file size, they can easily take over an hour to send. There is, however, a way to cut down on the size of large files – by compressing them.

Compressing files

Normally, every computer file contains information that can be squeezed into a smaller file. Compression works for files rather as shorthand works for text. A page of shorthand represents many pages of normal writing, and a compressed file can be many times smaller than the original file.

Files types vary in the extent to which they can be compressed. Some can be squeezed into a file a tenth of the size, but others may not show any noticeable difference. However, most types of document and image file – apart from GIF (image) files – can be compressed quite effectively. So if you want to send a large file to someone, it is a good idea to compress it before you attach it to a message – it will take you less time to send it, and less time for the recipient to download it.

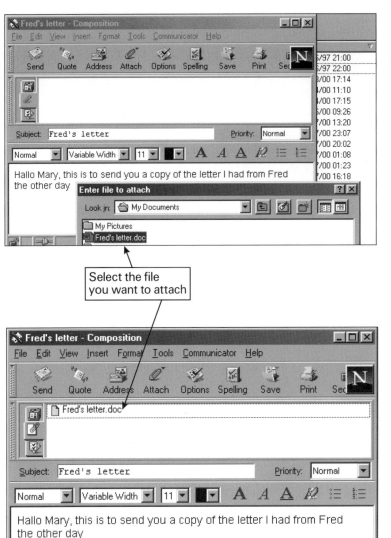

Fig. 25. Netscape Messenger: selecting a file to attach to an email. The file in question is called 'Fred's letter.doc'.

Select the file you want to attach

Fig. 26. The email composition window now shows the name of the attached file, 'Fred's letter.doc'.

Compression software

To compress a file, you need a compression software program. There are several versions of such software available, but one of the most popular, and most flexible, is WinZip.

WinZip
http://www.winzip.com
You can try WinZip for twenty-one days. After that, you must pay $29 if you want to continue using it. Once you install it, you can use WinZip on your computer from within Windows Explorer. WinZip compresses a file, or several files, into a single archive that has a 'ZIP' extension, for example:

myfiles.zip

Sending and receiving files ....

Fig. 27. WinZip is essential for anyone using the internet. It is a brilliant program that could save you pounds in telephone bills. Click on the file you want to unzip (in this case a file called c09.zip).

Fig. 28. Select a folder in which to place the unzipped file, then click Unzip Now to view its contents.

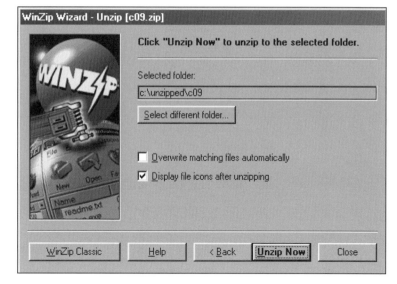

Freezip
http://www.n-media.com/zip.htm
Another common compression program is Freezip. This has the advantage, as its name indicates, of being free.

How to compress a file
This is how to compress a file using WinZip:

1. Open Windows Explorer.

2. Select the file or files you want to compress.

3. Open the File menu.

4. Select Add to Zip. This will start WinZip.

5. In WinZip, type a name for the compressed file, such as 'myfile'.

6. Click Add.

To send the zipped file by email, start a new email message as normal. Then attach the compressed file to your email, just as you would attach any other file to it.

Decompressing files

For recipients to be able to decompress compressed files ('archives'), they must have WinZip, or some other compatible program. Once they have the correct software, they should:

1. save the attachment in a folder somewhere on their computer (e.g. in My Documents)

2. decompress the file, using WinZip for example.

Of course, recipients need to have the program that the file is meant to be used with. The file will be useless to them otherwise. For example, if you send someone an Excel worksheet, they will need to have Microsoft Excel installed on their computer, or some other kind of software capable of reading read Excel worksheets. Equally, if you send them a document created in Word2000, they will be unable to read it if they have an earlier version of Word such as Word95, let alone a very old Microsoft word processing program such as MS Works.

This is not a problem with the most basic or common types of file such as plain text documents and popular image files such as GIFs and JPEGs. The recipient will have software on their Windows or Apple Mac computer easily capable of viewing these.

Breaking up large messages

Even after compression, some files will be too large to send by email in one piece. Indeed, some internet service providers set an upper limit on message size. Usually the limit is one megabyte per message.

Outlook Express
Fortunately, you can set up Outlook Express so that it will divide one large message into several smaller ones before sending. When these smaller messages are received, the recipient's mail client automatically reassembles them into one message. To set Outlook Express to break up messages:

1. Open the Tools menu.

2. Click Accounts.

3. Select the Mail tab.

4. Click Properties.

5. Select the Advanced tab.

6. Select the check box, 'Break apart messages larger than KB.'

7. Enter the maximum file size to accept before breaking them up.

Fig. 29. You can use Outlook Express to break up large messages before sending them. In this case, Outlook Express has been set to break up all messages larger than 60 kilobytes.

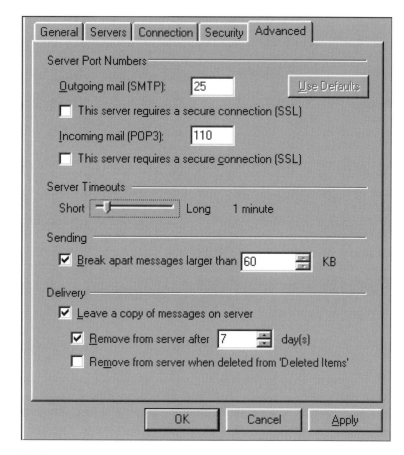

XferPro
http://ftp.pcworld.com/pub/system/other/xfpnt200.zip
XferPro is a useful utility for decoding files. You can obtain it from the PC World website, address as above.

The threat of viruses

A biological virus, such as the flu virus, is very small and highly infectious. It can multiply only in the living cells of animals, plants or bacteria. A computer virus is rather like this. It is a very small computer program that 'infects' computers by attaching itself to larger programs and certain types of document. All computer viruses are manmade. Even a simple virus can cause extensive and irreparable damage to equipment and data stored on computer systems.

Most viruses are designed to disrupt the normal operation of the computer or damage and delete files. The bit that causes the damage – the 'payload' – can be as harmless as a silly message on the screen, or as disastrous as a completely corrupted hard drive. The new strains of virus also spread themselves by email, using the addresses in your email client's address book.

Viruses must not be underestimated!

Fig. 30. Before disaster strikes in the form of a virus, get yourself some antivirus software, e.g. from Data Rescue, and learn how to use it properly.

Protecting against virus infection

A computer virus can easily destroy days, months or years of work, yet through ignorance or apathy we often fail to take sensible precautions. The mere mention of viruses puts fear into our hearts but not, it seems, into our minds. Even the most seasoned computer expert will occasionally ignore the advice that he gives, and loses valuable work he has not backed up. Perhaps, like many others, you fail to take precautions because:

1. You are too busy.

2. You have never experienced a virus in the past.

3. You think the risks are probably exaggerated.

4. You haven't got any antivirus software or, if you have, are uncertain how to use it.

Sending and receiving files ....

If you insert disks into your computer, receive email messages, share disks, or download files from the internet, you are likely to encounter viruses.

Taking the right precautions
The number one precaution you should take right now is to get hold of a virus-scanning program and commit yourself to updating it frequently. New viruses appear every day. There now are well over 40,000 different viruses and variations of them.

The precautions for most attachments (except Office documents, page 53) are simple but must be strictly followed:

1. Never open downloaded or attached files. Save them first.

2. Scan them with an up-to-date virus scanner before running or opening them. It may help if you create a special 'quarantine' directory or folder on your hard drive for this purpose.

3. You may have changed your browser's settings so that it can automatically open downloaded files. If so, disable it now. It may be a little inconvenient but it could save you hours of work, aggravation and heartache.

4. Back up all your files regularly. Keep the clearly labelled and dated backup disks or tapes in a safe place.

Antivirus software

Antivirus software is designed only to scan for the most common viruses. Therefore purchase anitvirus software that promises regular and frequent updates. And make sure you get those updates. If you do this – or better still if you use two scanners from different companies – you can be fairly certain that all known viruses will be detected.

Good antivirus software should:

1. Be up to date – you should obtain an update as soon as one is available.

2. Conform to standards set by the National Computer Security Association (NCSA).

3. Be able to scan floppy disks, hard drives, CD-ROMs and network drives.

4. Be able to monitor your computer while you are working, so that it can warn you if you try to open an infected file.

5. Include a version that can be run on a bootable floppy disk.

Where to obtain antivirus software
Antivirus software can be obtained from any computer retailer, on diskettes or CD-ROMs. Among the popular brands are McAfee and Dr Solomon's AntivirusToolkit.

Fig. 31. Dr Solomon's AntiVirus Toolkit is a well-known software package, from Symantec.

F-Prot
One of the best antivirus scanners is F-Prot, written by Fridrik Skulason in Iceland. It is available by email, and free for private use. To get the current version send email to the following address:

f-prot-update@complex.is

Type the following into the message body:

send-as: uue

It is also available from:

http://www.isvr.soton.ac.uk/ftp/pc/f-prot

Download.com
http://www.download.com
At this web site, you can download other free ant-virus software such as Disinfectant for Macintosh and trial versions of other commercial anti-virus software.

Sending and receiving files ....

Downloads for **PC** | Mac | Linux | Windows CE | PalmPilot

- Antivirus
- Backup
- Desktop Enhancements
- File & Disk Management
- File Compression
- Launchers
- Network

- Printers
- Screensavers
- Security & Encryption
- Shell & Desktop Management
- Start- up/Shutdown Screens

- *Most Popular*
- *New Releases*
- *Our Picks*

Scan your PC for software updates

Most Popular
Week ending May 28

Fig. 32. Download.com is one of the places which will have a good selection of antivirus software, and much more.

Most anti-virus software scans your computer's memory soon after you switch on. The software should give a warning if you try to open an infected file. Once an infected file is identified, most virus scanners will ask you if you want to clean the infected file or, if it cannot be cleaned, to delete it. Let the scanner clean or delete the infected file. Don't be tempted to ignore its existence or you will end up with many more infected files. Deleting is the safest option.

Above all, read the instructions that come with the antivirus software and follow them.

Macro viruses

Most documents can now incorporate special computer programs called macros. For example, you may have a word processor document, in which a macro automatically carries out some task when the document is opened. Virus writers have taken advantage of this, and written macro viruses that infect the macros contained in some documents.

Virus scanners can detect macro viruses once they have infected a document, but by then it may be too late. Make sure that your programs are set to warn you before running macros contained within documents. By default, Word and other Microsoft Office programs do display warning messages whenever you open a document that contains macros. You can then choose to allow the macros to run or open the document with its macros disabled. Many macros are safe but if you have any suspicions, scan the document for a virus.

Microsoft Word documents
To enable the macro protection in Microsoft Word 97, for example:

1. Start Word.

2. Open the Tools menu.

3. Select Options and select the General tab.

4. Click on Macro Virus Protection, and make sure it is checked. If you accidentally let a macro virus run even once, your system may have had the virus detection turned off.

If you have macro protection turned on, there should be no damage. However, one further step you can take to minimise the risk is to prevent Office documents from automatically opening by adjusting the settings in Windows Explorer (not to be confused with Internet Explorer!):

1. Double-click the icon My Computer, on your desktop.

2. Click on the View menu.

3. Click Folder Options

Fig. 33. Here's where Microsoft Word should be adjusted so that your computer asks your permission before running downloaded files. We're talking about the risk of macro viruses here.

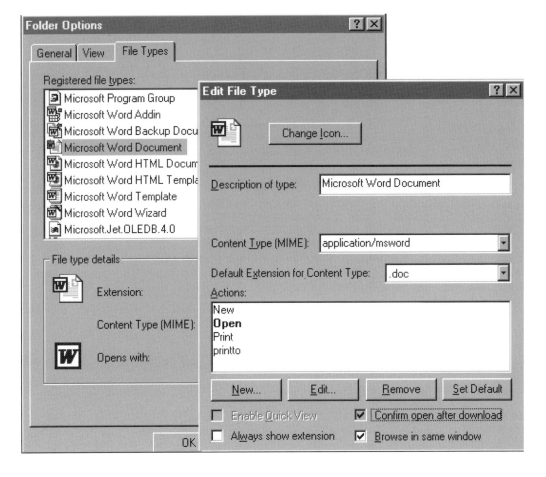

55

4. Click the File Types tab. Scroll down the list of file types and look for any reference to Office programs such as Microsoft Word or Excel. Then, with each:

5. Select the entry.

6. Click the Edit button.

7. Check the 'Confirm open after download' option.

That will prevent Office documents opening automatically in Internet Explorer or Outlook Express when viewed. Flaws do exist which might allow a malicious macro to run without warning, even if you did have the macro virus protection turned on. For more information see:

http://www.microsoft.com/security

These have not been generally exploited, but all it needs is one virus to get through and it might have turned the macro-virus protection off.

Microsoft has released a patch that does practically the same as the steps above. It will ensure that opening any Office document – Word, Excel, PowerPoint or Access – from Internet Explorer will cause a warning to be displayed. You can download this patch from:

http://officeupdate.microsoft.com/downloadDetails/confirm.htm

Myths

If you receive a virus warning by email, think twice before panicking. Virus hoaxes far outnumber genuine warnings and, besides wasting your time, they can be a cause of severe embarrassment to the internet newcomer. How do you identify a hoax? There are several signs:

1. If the warning sounds as if it is has been sent by an official organisation or uses technical terms, it is probably a hoax because that kind of organisation rarely sends virus warnings to individuals unless they are part of a newsletter or mailing list.

2. If the warning urges you to pass it on to your friends, it is probably a hoax.

3. Also, if the warning says that it is a Federal Communication Commission (FCC) warning, it is a hoax. The FCC has not sent, and never will send, warnings on viruses.

Always doublecheck before embarrassing yourself and clogging up the internet. A useful website to look at is Computer Virus Myths:

Computer Virus Myths
http://www.kumite.com/myths
This contains descriptions of many known hoaxes.

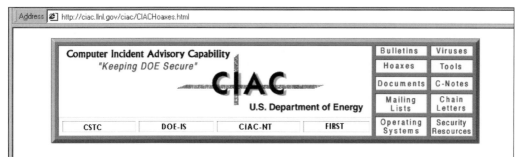

Address 🔗 http://ciac.llnl.gov/ciac/CIACHoaxes.html

Computer Incident Advisory Capability				Bulletins	Viruses
"Keeping DOE Secure"				Hoaxes	Tools
CIAC				Documents	C-Notes
				Mailing Lists	Chain Letters
		U.S. Department of Energy		Operating Systems	Security Resources
CSTC	DOE-IS	CIAC-NT	FIRST		

Internet Hoaxes

Please Note:

This web site is provided as a public service; however, CIAC does not have the resources to investigate and/or confirm every hoax currently circulating the Internet. CIAC appreciates input on questionable hoaxes, but we are not able to respond back to each e-mail message. You can help eliminate "junk mail" by educating the public on how to identify a new hoax warning, how to identify a valid warning and what to do

Fig. 34. Not all virus warnings are true, though. If you receive a warning by email, it is far more likely to be a hoax. Check it out on a site like CIAC.

CIAC
http://ciac.llnl.gov/ciac/CIACHoaxes.html
This is another site worth checking out for internet hoaxes. CIAC stands for Computer Incident Advisory Capability.

5 Social email

In this chapter we will explore:

▶ *taking part – internet mailing lists*
▶ *playing games by email*

Taking part: internet mailing lists

It is quite easy to send an email message to a group of people. You just add all their addresses to the message and send it to the whole group. If another person in the group wants to send a reply to the group, that person can reply to the original message, or send a new one, including all of the members' email addresses.

Both Outlook Express and Netscape Messenger have a Reply All button. If you click this, it will add all the email addresses contained in a group email. Using this button, you can reply to all of the 'members' of the group of recipients and so take part in a group discussion. This is a simple forum or mailing list.

You can extend this group idea by using a mailing list administered by a list server:

▶ *Mailing list* – An internet forum in which messages are distributed by email to the members of the forum. There are two types of lists, discussion and announcement. Discussion lists allow exchange between list members. Announcement lists are one-way only and used to distribute information such as news or humour.

▶ *List server* – This is a computer program that manages the list of members and the flow of messages in a mailing list. The list server is usually installed on the computer system of an organisation like a university or an internet service provider.

Using mailing lists is simple. In essence, you take the following steps:

1. Find a mailing list of interest to you.

2. Subscribe (sign up) to it.

3. Set up filters to manage the flow of incoming messages.

4. Read and reply to the messages which interest you.

And if you wish to leave a list:

5. Unsubscribe, in other words sign off.

Liszt, the mailing list directory

IMAGE

Since the 1970s, people have been joining "mailing lists" to talk about their favorite topics via e-mail! Check out our intro if you're new. We've also got a Usenet newsgroups directory and an IRC chat directory, if you want to make even more friends.

Most recent update: 26 new lists added to Liszt Select on February 23, 2000

Liszt has joined forces with Topica! Read all about it in this letter from Scotty.

I. **Search Liszt's main directory of 90,095 mailing lists:**   [   ] go [help]

Junk Filtering: ○ none ● some ○ lots

GO Express Network Search   *Find groups matching:* [all these words ▼]

II. **...or click on any topic to browse** Liszt Select: Arts (206 lists)
Crafts Television Movies

http://www.liszt.com/

Liszt
http://www.liszt.com
Perhaps the best site for information about mailing lists is Liszt – take care with the spelling! This is a very large and well-established directory of internet discussion groups. Liszt contains details of a staggering 90,000 different internet mailing lists, covering every topic under the sun, and lots of other discussion-type contacts besides.

Reference.com
http://www.reference.com
Reference.com is another site that allows you to search mailing lists. Aside from searching in the normal way, you can also submit an Active Query. This will keep working for you, even when you are not online. Reference.com will remember your query and run it periodically. As soon as something appears that matches your query, you will be sent a notification by email. For example, if the tickets are sold out for your favourite football team, you might want to receive the first messages that talk about ticket sales for your team.

Tile.Net Lists
http://tile.net/lists/
This web site is a functional reference point leading to thousands of different email discussion lists, announcement lists and information lists available on the internet. The individual lists are listed by name, description, and domain, or you can do a keyword search to find lists that deal with a particular topic.

Fig. 35. If you are looking to join an internet mailing list, Liszt is one of the oldest and best directories of such lists around.

Social email..

Before you subscribe to a discussion group, make sure it's the sort of thing you want. As well as using a directory like Liszt, you should also be able to find information from a list server itself. List servers usually host many different mailing lists. To find specific information you need to specify the name of the list, once you have found a likely one from Liszt or some other source.

Try sending an email to the list server, with the words 'info [listname]' in the body of your message. For example, if the name of the list you want information about is 'webtoday-l', you would type the following line into the body of the your email message:

info webtoday-l

The directories will contain the list server addresses for each mailing list or alternative instructions.

Subscribing to an email list

Once you have found one or more lists that you wish to join, you can instruct its server to add you to the list. This is called subscribing to the list, and means you can start receiving messages. Once you subscribe, you will start receiving the messages from the list automatically.

A subscription request has to be worded in a certain way in order for it to work. Usually it has to be in the form 'subscribe listname' where list-name is the name of the mailing list you are interested in. You email this request to the list server.

When you subscribe to a list, your name and email address is automatically added to the list. You will receive a standard letter of welcome (via email) with further information about the list. From that time on, you will receive all mail (posts) sent to the list by its members. You can join in the discussions anytime or simply read them. If you respond, you can send your response to the list address, mentioned in the welcome letter, so that all members of the list will receive it, or to an individual on the list. Don't confuse the list server's address with the mailing list address. The list address is the one that you use – once you have subscribed – to send and receive messages to other people on the list. The server's address is simply a computer address used to send commands or requests to the list server.

▶ *Try this* – Experiment by getting a daily review of general interest web sites sent to you. Send a message to 'majordomo@web-today.net' with the words 'subscribe webtoday-l' (small L) in the body of your message. Do not put anything in the subject line of your message. Note that majordomo@web-today.net is the address of the list server.

You may then receive a message asking you to confirm that you actually want to receive the reviews. This confirmation is designed to protect you being swamped by messages from a mailing list should someone forge your address.

You may also receive a message that your subscription is being for-

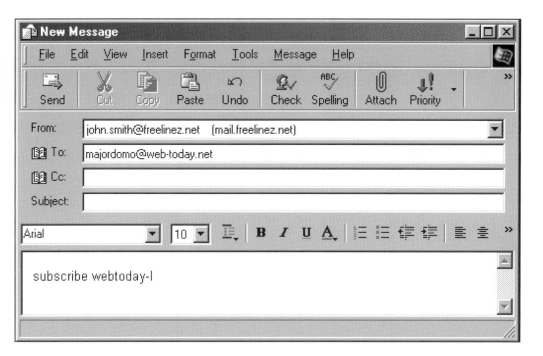

Fig. 36. Subscribing by email to a mailing list called WebToday.

warded to the list owner for approval. Some lists have waiting lists, or are selective about who may subscribe. If your request is forwarded for approval, the list owner should contact you with a request for confirmation something like the following:

Someone (possibly you) has requested that your email address be added to or deleted from the mailing list "webtoday-l@web-today.-net".

If you really want this action to be taken, please send the following commands (exactly as shown) back to "Majordomo@web-today.-net":

auth 2415c3c0 subscribe webtoday-l

If you do not want this action to be taken, simply ignore this message and the request will be disregarded.

You should reply to the message in the way that it tells you to. In this particular case, you will need to send an email with the following line in the message:

auth 2415c3c0 subscribe webtoday-l

Soon after you send the confirmation, you should receive an introductory message containing instructions on using the list and its policies.

Social email

Save the message for future reference, because it will also contain instructions for unsubscribing. If you lose it, send a message to the server with the words 'intro webtoday-l' in the body. An introductory message will look like this:

Welcome to the webtoday-l mailing list!

Please save this message for future reference. Thank you.

If you ever want to remove yourself from this mailing list, send the following command in email to

< webtoday-l-request@web-today.net > :

    unsubscribe

Or you can send mail to ‹Majordomo@web-today.net› with the following command in the body of your email message:

    unsubscribe webtoday-l

or from another account, besides you@yourisp.co.uk:

    unsubscribe webtoday-l you@yourisp.co.uk

At some point, you may need to get in contact with the owner of the list – for example, if you have trouble unsubscribing or have questions about the list itself. In this case, send email to:

owner-webtoday-l@web-today.net

This is the general rule for most mailing lists when you need to contact a human.

Once you have received this message, you are subscribed to the list and you should start to receive daily site reviews. Subscribing to most other lists is done in the same way.

If for some reason you wish to have the mailings sent to a different address – for example, a friend's address or one of your other accounts – you add that address to the command. Suppose you are sending a request from work, but wish to receive webtoday-l mail at your home account, for which we will use you@yourisp.co.uk as an example. In this case you would put the line:

subscribe listname you@yourisp.co.uk

▶ *Commands* – Don't worry if you can't remember the right commands. Most list servers are automatically set up to send out further information about them. Send the list server a message with no subject, and just the word HELP in the body of your message.

Once you have subscribed to a mailing list, it would be a good idea to set up a filter that separates the mailing list messages from your normal email. Some mailing lists generate hundreds of messages every day and could soon swamp your other incoming mail.

Filtering messages

You may well start to have large volumes of incoming email if you sub-scribe to a popular mailing list. Fortunately most email programs, such as Outlook Express and Netscape Messenger, can help you to manage all these emails more efficiently. For example, you can very easily use filtering 'rules' to sort messages from a mailing list into different folders.

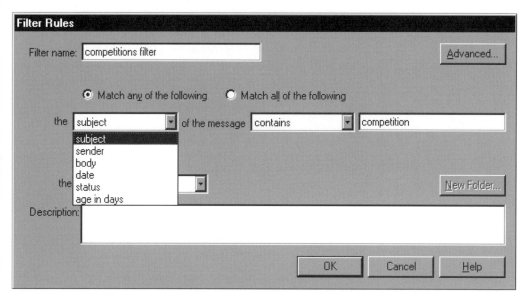

Most email programs allow the use of filters. The criteria you use to filter messages can be any part of the incoming messages or articles:

Fig. 37. Rules, or filters, make email more manageable – especially if you intend to subscribe to one or more mailing lists.

1. who the message is to

2. who it is from

3. what the subject contains

4. what the body text contains

Some email clients and newsreaders (software for reading messages in newsgroups) allow you to set multiple filters which can look at different parts of a message and carry out a variety of tasks depending on what they find. For example, if you receive a message from a mailing list, you could have the email program automatically move it to a special folder. Similarly, if it is from a certain person on that list, the email program could mark it in colour to attract your attention. See also pages 37 and 39.

Unsubscribing

When you want to stop the mailing list sending you messages, you will need to send a message to the list server with a particular line in the body of your message. This line is usually:

signoff listname

or

unsubscribe listname

where listname is the name of the list, for example:

unsubscribe webtoday-l

Try it yourself. After a couple of days of receiving the reviews from webto-day-l, unsubscribe by sending mail to the same address. Remember to avoid putting in a subject line, and to type 'unsubscribe webtoday-l' in the body of the message. Even if you find the reviews interesting, unsub-scribe just for practice. You can always subscribe again later.

Other listserve commands

So far, you have learned the useful skills of how to join and leave a list, and how to ask for help and general information. Certain other commands may, or may not, be useful to you at some time. These are:

SET

REVIEW

Fig. 38. Sending an email
to unsubscribe from Web
Today.

CONCEAL

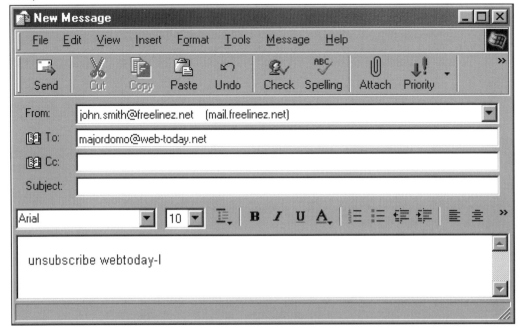

Whenever you send a message to a list server, you receive an acknowledgement after the message has been received. Some acknowledgements can be quite long and tedious. You can control the amount of acknowledgement you receive from a list by sending an email message to the mailing list address with the following line in the body of your message:

SET listname option

Listname is the name of the list, and option can be: ACK, NOACK, or MSGACK.

1.   ACK provides mail acknowledgement.

2.   MSGACK provides acknowledgement of command messages only.

3.   NOACK stops all acknowledgements.

Sending an email message to the mailing list address with the following line in the body of the message will provide you with the network address and name of all the list's subscribers:

REVIEW listname

Sending an email message to the mailing list address with the following line in the body of the message will hide your name from users issuing the REVIEW command:

SET listname CONCEAL

Playing games by email

Games involving action, such as shooting everything in site or flying a flight simulator, would be impossible to PBEM (play by email). However, email is perfect for board games or games involving a puzzle of some kind. War strategy and role-playing games dominate the email game world but there are plenty of other types. They range from *Lotto* to *British Internet Soccer*, *Murder on the Orient Express* mysteries and *Adventures with Star Trek*.

One of the better PBEM organisations is Richard's Play-By-eMail Server. Richard offers eighteen varieties of chess, three of backgammon, six of checkers and umpteen other board-like games. For full instructions, send an email with HELP in the subject line to:

pbmserv@gamerz.net

To find a PBEM organisation you could try a general search engine such as AltaVista or Yahoo!. However, there is a site dedicated to email, and to snail-mail games such as PBM (Play by Mail), at:

http://www.pbm.com/ ~ lindahl/pbm.html

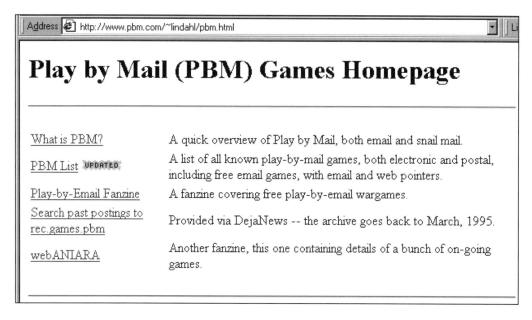

Play by Mail (PBM) Games Homepage

What is PBM?	A quick overview of Play by Mail, both email and snail mail.
PBM List **UPDATED**	A list of all known play-by-mail games, both electronic and postal, including free email games, with email and web pointers.
Play-by-Email Fanzine	A fanzine covering free play-by-email wargames.
Search past postings to rec.games.pbm	Provided via DejaNews -- the archive goes back to March, 1995.
webANIARA	Another fanzine, this one containing details of a bunch of on-going games.

Fig. 39. Email games are a good way to pass some of that time while the boss is away, and easier to hide than hearts or FreeCell.

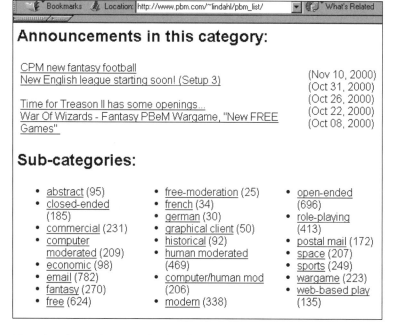

Announcements in this category:

CPM new fantasy football	(Nov 10, 2000)
New English league starting soon! (Setup 3)	(Oct 31, 2000)
	(Oct 26, 2000)
Time for Treason II has some openings...	(Oct 22, 2000)
War Of Wizards - Fantasy PBeM Wargame, "New FREE Games"	(Oct 08, 2000)

Sub-categories:

- abstract (95)
- closed-ended (185)
- commercial (231)
- computer moderated (209)
- economic (98)
- email (782)
- fantasy (270)
- free (624)

- free-moderation (25)
- french (34)
- german (30)
- graphical client (50)
- historical (92)
- human moderated (469)
- computer/human mod (206)
- modern (338)

- open-ended (696)
- role-playing (413)
- postal mail (172)
- space (207)
- sports (249)
- wargame (223)
- web-based play (135)

Yoyodyne is another organisation that specialises in online games. Send a blank email to the following address for further information:

win@yoyo.com

6 Your email privacy

In this chapter we will explore:

▶ *your emails at work or college*
▶ *the problem of file deletion*
▶ *some tips for employees*
▶ *PGP encryption*
▶ *using anonymous email*
▶ *using remailers*
▶ *anonymous web-based email*

. . . .

Your emails at work or college

Have you been allocated a personal email address at your school, college, university, or place of work? Before you think of sending and receiving messages using this email for private purposes, take a moment to reflect. An increasing number of institutions and organisations today track all their students and employees as they use the internet. Indeed, they can (and do) use sophisticated software specially designed to automatically scan all email messages, incoming and outgoing. Some problem areas include:

1. playing games by email

2. sending or receiving pornography

3. sending or receiving messages which may cause discredit or damage to the organisation, or threaten confidential matters

4. students trying to obtain readymade material to plagiarise for project work

5. wasting time and money on non-essential communications

The problem of file deletion

There are many examples of people losing their job or being removed from their place of study when a careless word or two in an email message fell into the wrong hands. Deleting an email message is no protection.

What is meant by deletion?
'Deleting' a computer file simply marks as free the disk space occupied by that file. However, it leaves all the original information on the hard disk until it happens to get overwritten by another file. A person with even a little computer knowledge can easily read the information in that file, using a popular and inexpensive program such as Norton Utilities.

Your email privacy ....

Network file storage

If your computer is on a company or university network, you could throw the thing into a furnace and there would still be a record of your email messages. Messages and other files are routinely stored and backed up in a central location on organisation networks.

The risks of a shared work environment

It is understandable if an organisation monitors your email traffic and web activities. Employers, for example, practically own you, after all! But it is not just your employer who is likely to be snooping on you. Office rivalry from colleagues can become intense, and the temptation for a rival to snoop on your work or 'put the boot in' can sometimes become irresistible.

Once a person logs on with your username and password, they can access all of your email messages from any computer on the network. Keep your password very close to your chest – not stuck to your computer monitor – and change it from time to time.

Some tips for employees

There is little you can really do to keep your email private at work. However, there are one or two precautions you can take:

1. Don't put anything in an email that you would not want any of the following to see: the boss, a solicitor, a judge or magistrate, the police, investigators, auditors, your colleagues, superiors and subordinates, a competing company – in short, anybody apart from the person you intend to send it to.

2. Don't assume that just because you send an email to a trusted friend, other, less friendly, people will not read it. The recipient of a message may not be as careful with information as you are, or may not be as friendly towards you as you think.

3. Think before you get angry by email. Don't open yourself to problems, or prosecution, just because of a thoughtless or rash remark. The same applies to talking about your company – never discuss sensitive company information.

4. Treat your computer passwords like your house keys. Don't make them too simple, don't leave them lying around (on bits of paper), and remember to change them occasionally.

5. If you insist on leaving a password lying around, at least make it a *wrong* password. That way you might catch someone out.

In short, be as discreet as you would be when having a discussion in a busy restaurant where you can be observed by many people and overheard by some of them.

PGP encryption

PGP International
http://www.pgpi.com
Probably the most secure way to send a private email is to use Pretty Good Privacy or PGP. This is a highly respected, state-of-the-art form of encryption, available free to everyone. A hacker group wrote about the difficulty of breaking a message encoded with PGP: 'If you had 1,000,000,000 machines that could try 1,000,000,000 keys/sec, it would still take all these machines longer than the universe as we know it has existed, and then some, to find the key.' Civilian experts have been trying to break public key cryptography since 1978 without success.

Fig. 40. Using PGP (Pretty Good Privacy) is the best way to encrypt your email messages so they can be truly private.

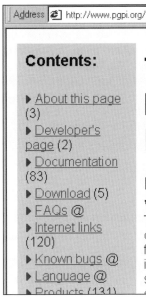

Address 🦋 http://www.pgpi.org/

Contents:

▶ About this page (3)
▶ Developer's page (2)
▶ Documentation (83)
▶ Download (5)
▶ FAQs @
▶ Internet links (120)
▶ Known bugs @
▶ Language @
▶ Products (131)

The International PGP Home Page

Download the latest **version**

The PGP download wizard lets you download the latest freeware PGP version for your platform, whether you want the international or the US variant. It also shows you where to buy the latest commercial version for your platform and

PGP is such a good system that some countries such as the USA, Canada and Japan classify it as a weapon. Until recently, this has made it as difficult to export some forms of PGP as it is to export grenades or ground-to-air missiles.

Phil Zimmerman, the creator of the system, completed PGP just as rumours were coming out of Washington that strong encryption could be outlawed. Realising that PGP would be included in such a ban, he released the source code free of charge. Friends of his also published the code on the internet, making it available to the whole world overnight. Zimmerman was soon told that he was under investigation by the FBI for 'illegal arms trafficking'. In releasing PGP onto the internet, he gave the ordinary person in the street the ability to send messages that could remain private even when under attack by the most powerful and well-equipped intelligence services. The debate about whether he is a public hero or an anarchist continues.

What is PGP?
Most forms of encryption are based on a key of some kind. One of the

simplest codes used on the internet is ROTT 13, which is sometimes used to keep unsuitable messages from being read by young children. In this code each letter in a message is substituted for the one thirteen places after it. The letter A is substituted by N, the letter B by O, and so on. For example, the message:

Kye's birthday present is under the bed

becomes:

Xlr'f oveguqnl cerfrag vf haqre gur orq

Clearly, only the youngest cybersnoop would be fooled by such simple encryption.

ROTT 13 uses a key – namely 13 – to encrypt a message. Since everyone (except the young children it is meant to protect) knows the key, it is said to be a 'public key'. PGP also uses public keys but the keys themselves, and the way they are used, are far more complex. And PGP uses not only the public key but also a second, private, key. These two complementary keys – called a key pair – are used in combination to encrypt a message. If you use PGP, you must first use the software to create a key pair before you can begin exchanging encrypted email with other PGP users.

How to send emails using PGP
To send someone a PGP-encrypted email message, you use a copy of that person's public key to encrypt the message. That person then unlocks it with their private key. When someone sends you an encrypted message, they use a copy of your public key to encrypt the data, and only you can unlock the message by using your private key.

It can be explained in a simple way by comparing your public key with a set of identical padlocks (the public keys). You own a set of brand new, high quality padlocks. You give each of your friends and business associates one of these padlocks. When they send you a box of goodies, they first lock it using your padlock. Once the box is closed, the box can only be opened with your key (the private key). Giving your public key away is not a risk to you: the padlock itself is useless to anybody unless they are sending something to you because only you can open the padlock once it is closed.

Once a person has a copy of your public key – unlike a padlock which has to be sent back to them each time – they can use it over and over again whenever they want to send you a PGP message. Public keys are just blocks of text, so you can easily send them by ordinary email.

Key servers
Public keys can also be made 'public' in a more literal sense. They can be published on the internet on special computers/web sites called key servers. If someone wants to send you a secure message but does not have your public key, they can obtain a copy from a key server.

▶ *Key server* - A computer on the internet, the main function of which is to store people's public PGP keys.

If you do not encrypt your internet communications, it is a simple matter for an attacker to intercept your messages, especially email. If you use PGP correctly, the attacker will have to expend massively greater effort and expense in trying to gain access to your information.

An example of a public key
Version: PGPfreeware 6.0.2i.

```
XTEfEeGCJ6Z2vhXV52xChY426zJCHHHUa5N/fGHh2ar0eINR
RVOsTmEIuEfGzAcjRYEdqYAuAsBqybpLZcpqXyaJpKZbdRmW
rrvKuzjBabz/bq4lb7geU/dCsu2cOrPUS2TsvFU/7bxLm95Y+Ra
Ui4lekhzCx1UB4ZOlbvTIZizoRIF4D2fQiQBGBBgRAgAGBQI26
0WRAAoJEB0A3siK2Yc8xRoAoLExr+t4UZVLg4ISzbnGn4JHt1
YzAJ4rNdYZQFnanwzfRHJWR7nevc+hgw===u43AmQGiBD
brRZERBADzuw1Fw1f1ddbeujSZDAP19fsKCz+QFgshDLMOVd
+LNkPoB9aOh6wQKX4WK1/7oWMZ3FLAO1NjXcbqW7Uva9fb
QzdpTo1pG7uJNgw+CED55zd6QOYJBYDCWy0fxBFf7GGrSzx
wZdJk49WnyeNYOgjt2rBrGNcTqDPaENh3U3j2PwCg/+PVZX
9x2Uk89PY3bzpnhV5JZzf24rnRPxfx2vIPFRzBhznzJZv8VDS2
nyOFQI+jqyIDmmWAz8JTPFdtdwDIdMc2rpQ71FQhSlpKDyBp
NPKQoDE3mv9PEhKPbw7Bze+hTSYCX6RuRJfoWOFLNEl7qku
sRGEnqJ9
```

Making sure your keys are secure
Here are some essential precautions to take that will ensure that your keys are secure. If someone breaks into your house, all of your efforts with PGP will come to nothing if your passphrases or keys are easily accessible. Don't leave either on a scrap of paper or in a plain text file on your computer. This is also vital if you are using a computer at work or working on a shared computer.

Just because you use PGP, it would be a mistake to feel that you are invulnerable. Cryptography can only protect data while it is encrypted. If someone gains access to your computer, they will still be able to get hold of any unencrypted information.

▶ *Passphrase* – This is like a password but more secure because it uses many more letters and is therefore much more difficult to guess or work out.

PGP is not designed to protect your data while it is in plain text form on a compromised system. Nor can it prevent an intruder from using sophisticated measures to read your private key while it is being used. You will have to recognise these risks on multi-user systems and adjust your expectations and behaviour accordingly. Perhaps your situation is such that you should consider only running PGP on an isolated single-user system under your direct physical control.

The length of your keys is also a factor. Keys are basically very big numbers. Key size is measured in bits. The number representing a 1024-bit key is mind-bogglingly huge. In public key cryptography, the bigger the key, the more secure the encoded message. A key length of 40 bits offers poor security, but 1024 bits would keep out the most persistent and powerful attacker.

PGP is at the forefront of a new war between private users and governments. PGP can protect the rights to privacy of normal users as well as protect the privacy of criminals.

Using anonymous email

Let's say you are a clerk or a manager working for a large company and you realise that the boss is causing an environmental health risk. You know that if you inform the authorities by email, you will probably be found out and lose your job or worse. What do you do? Or suppose you are a student who wants to tell the rest of the world that animal experiments are being performed in your department on domestic cats. Several other students have been expelled after having talked to the media. How do you get the word out without being identified?

Normally it is very easy to identify the sender of an email message or a Usenet post – far easier than it is for a normal letter. The header of an email message contains information that can identify you to others, and contains information about the route that the message took across the internet.

So how do you make your email anonymous? With snail mail it's easy – just omit your return address. If you want a reply, you can use a PO Box number for replies. With email, though, the answer is to use an anonymous remailer.

Using remailers

An anonymous remailer is a special kind of internet computer service. It allows you to send an email message, or Usenet post, without revealing your identity to anyone who reads or intercepts the message – including the recipient if need be. Some remailers also permit you to send email while protecting your email records from your internet service provider.

Anonymous mailing services preserve your privacy by acting as a go-between when you send messages. Such services might slow your internet experience, but if you need anonymity any time, it is a small price to pay.

There are basically three types of remailers:

1. pseudo-anonymous
2. cypherpunk
3. mixmaster

Pseudo-anonymous remailers
Imagine you work for a company called Brown Sludge Chemicals. You have a friend in a similar company called Acrid Smoke Products. To discuss the extent of pollution by your employers before reporting them to the press, you might decide to use a remailer. The remailer would strip off

the real name and address from your message and replace it with dummy information before forwarding the message on to your friend. If your friend replies to the message, the remailer will similarly strip out his name, thus protecting everyone's privacy. Nobody is sacked.

It works as follows: you open an account with an operator; you will have to trust the operator not to reveal your identity, the content of your messages, or their destinations. The concept is based on trust, not real anonymity.

This example contains weaknesses, though. Messages can be tracked going in and coming out of the remailer. If only one remailer is used, the remailer operator knows both the originating and final addresses. Also, unless the message is encrypted, the remailer operator will know the content of the message.

Your company could track your messages up to the remailer, and then track outgoing messages that coincide with your message. Even though the identities may have changed, the size of the message in bytes will not. If it intercepts the message that comes out of the remailer immediately after yours goes in, your employer might be able to track your message and discover the recipient.

Alternatively, your employer could try to bring pressure on the remailer operator to divulge the information. Often a government has managed to force a remailer operator to divulge information about one of its users. A large company might wield enough power to do the same.

Cypherpunk remailers are far more secure than pseudo-anonymous remailers. Unfortunately, they are also much harder to use. but they are the next step up in the security hierarchy and are appropriate for people who are very serious about their anonymity.

Cypherpunk remailers

To understand how cypherpunk remailers send a message, imagine sending a parcel secretly to someone. The wrapping paper is a layer of encryption; the enclosed present is the message. Let's use two remailers

Fig. 41. ZipLip uses strong encryption on your messages. Web-based systems like this also mean that you can send private emails while you travel.

for simplicity.

You wrap the parcel up in three layers of paper. You have labelled each layer with the address of the next person in a chain. The outer layer also has your return address.

1. You 'send' the wrapped (encrypted) message to the first person, e.g. John (the first remailer).

2. John takes a layer of paper off and puts it in a file. He reads the name of the next person, Jane (the second remailer). He delivers the parcel to her, after adding his return address to the wrapping.

3. Jane receives the parcel. She knows it is from John, but she does not know that you are the original sender. John has removed the wrapper with your address (the email header information).

4. Jane now removes the next layer of paper. She files it and reads the name of the recipient of the parcel (Jackie). Jane delivers it to Jackie after adding her own return address to the wrapper.

5. Jackie now removes the final layer and opens the present, which is a box of chocolate from a secret admirer.

Now, Jackie can reply to the admirer even though she does not know his identity or address. She sends her reply to Jane's return address. Jane then sends it to John's return address, and he in turn sends it to your return address. Each person who handles the parcel, apart from you and the recipient Jackie, is a remailer.

Cypherpunk remailers send messages wrapped in a number of encrypted layers. Each remailer in the link removes a layer of encryption and follow the next set of instructions to sends the message on to the next destination. Each remailer only knows the identity of the next link in the chain.

If you want maximum privacy, you should send your message through two or more remailers. If done properly, you can ensure that *nobody* (no remailer operator or any snooper) can read both your real name and your message. This is the real meaning of anonymous. In practice, nobody can force a single anonymous remailer operator to reveal both identities, because the operator has no clue who you are! There is a slight possibility that two remailer operators will collaborate and reveal your identity, but using three or more links in the chain makes it a truly awesome task to try to identify both the sender and recipient. But is not impossible.

Messages can still be traced through the chain, because the remailers often forward a message straight away. The tracked message arrives and another leaves soon after. Presumably this is the same message with a different header and level of encryption. Anyone monitoring the traffic might rightly assume that it is the same message, and so track the second message to the next link in the chain. This may also be done long after the messages have been relayed if the remailer has logged the emails.

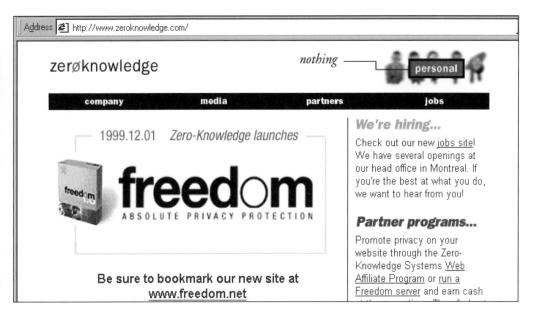

Address 🔲 http://www.zeroknowledge.com/

zerøknowledge

nothing ——— personal

company   media   partners   jobs

1999.12.01 *Zero-Knowledge launches*

freedom
ABSOLUTE PRIVACY PROTECTION

Be sure to bookmark our new site at www.freedom.net

We're hiring...
Check out our new jobs site!
We have several openings at
our head office in Montreal. If
you're the best at what you do,
we want to hear from you!

Partner programs...
Promote privacy on your
website through the Zero-
Knowledge Systems Web
Affiliate Program or run a
Freedom server and earn cash

One way of tracing messages through a chain of remailers is to capture a single message and send lots of identical copies of it to the remailer. The remailer will then send lots of identical messages to the next destination. Anyone tracking these messages will be able to identify the route and destination of the message. The process can then be repeated at each link in the chain.

Another class of remailer, the mixmaster, overcomes some of the weaknesses of cypherpunk remailers.

Fig. 42. Zero Knowledge produces a program called Freedom, which provides private communication over the internet. The firm is deluged by worried Americans who would rather trust a Canadian solution than their own government.

Mixmasters
The mixmaster remailing system relies on a special message format. All messages are identical in size, or broken up into identically sized packets. They also contain information that prevents an attacker replaying copies of a message. Each packet contains 20 headers; each time a header is stripped, the packet is bulked up again with random junk to the correct size.

Using mixmaster remailers is very complicated at present. It is beyond the needs of all but the most endangered people, or those in extremely sensitive situations. If you really need to maintain your privacy to that extent, see:

http://obscura.com/ ~ loki/index.cgi

Anonymous web-based email

See the next chapter for information about two well-known web-based privacy services: Anonymizer and Hushmail.

Other Internet Handbooks to help you

Your Privacy on the Internet, Kye Valongo (Internet Handbooks).

7 Email on the move

In this chapter we will explore:

▶ *web email access*
▶ *web-based private email*
▶ *using your existing email mailbox*
▶ *checking your mail server details*

If you are going to be on the road for a while, you may still want to keep in touch with your family or friends on the other side of the country or world. Email is the ideal way.

Web email access

Unless you carry around a laptop PC, you will need to find some way to get onto the web to use web-based email services such as Hotmail.

Hotmail
http://www.hotmail.com
Hotmail is a very popular web based email service owned and operated by Microsoft. It offers free email accounts in exchange for placing banner advertising on some of its pages. All messages in your Hotmail account are stored in a central location which you can access at any time over the internet, using a password of your choice. It currently offers 2 megabytes of storage space – more than enough for most users. The service is offered to individuals who are at least 18 years old, and to minors who have parental permission to open and maintain an account. You cannot

Fig. 43. Hotmail, owned and operated by Microsoft, is one of the most widely used web-based email services available.

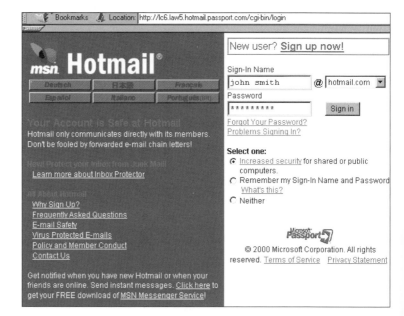

use your Hotmail address as a primary business address. If, however, you work for a company with which you have an email address and you want to use your Hotmail account to send and receive email while away from your computer at work, you can. You should read through Hotmail's detailed FAQs, privacy statement and terms of service before you sign up. You will be asked to complete a detailed online registration form.

Be on the lookout for different physical locations where you can access the internet. These include:

1. cybercafés which, for a small fee, typically offer access to the internet in slots of half an hour or an hour

2. web terminals (many international airports have pay-per-minute terminals you can use to access the web)

3. public libraries and business libraries

4. school, college and university libraries

5. friends with internet connections

Web-based email addresses are perfect for travellers, since you can use any web browser to access and reply to your messages. Using web-based email is simple: you just visit the host site, for example the Hotmail home page, log on and collect your mail. Most of the major search engines now offer free web-based email such as:

AltaVista
http://www.altavista.digital.com/

Yahoo!
http://www.yahoo.com

Fig. 44. Yahoo! is one of the many directory services that is now offering free web-based email – a neat solution provided that privacy is not your major concern.

Address ://edit.yahoo.com/config/mail?&i=IWZkZHNKlXRznNydEpidXV4dSF0ZEq0ZHh4fH5iU356YmNYcnM%3d&.rand=0.42845319014   Lir

YAHOO! Mail®

Yahoo!

Welcome to Yahoo! Mail

I'm a New User

Sign me up!

I'm already registered with Yahoo!

Yahoo! ID: [   ]
Password: [   ]

☐ Remember my ID & Password (What's this?)

[Sign in]

Trouble signing in?

Want mail? Sign up for Yahoo! Mail. It's free!

- Get your own **Yahoo!** email address.
- Access email from anywhere.
- You'll be registered with all of Yahoo!'s services.
- Get instant notification when you have new messages with Yahoo! Messenger

Yahoo! Mail for International Users

Europe : Danmark - France - Deutschland - Italia - España - Sverige - UK - Ireland - Norge
Pacific Rim : Australia - NZ - Hong Kong - Japan - Korea - Singapore - Taiwan - China

Web-based private email

Web-based email is also a way to make it more difficult for your IT manager reading your mail. You can often use a web-based email service to send mail, even if your company's firewall has disabled the email package in your browser. And if you want to check your home email account while at your desk, any one of the Check POP mail services can help.

If you need to be anonymous, for instance if you wish to visit a site like Alcoholics Anonymous, you can stay more or less hidden behind a free email service. You can choose an identity totally unrelated to your real name. In this way, nobody will be able to find out who you are. Several internet services specialise in helping people to keep their identities secret. The better known ones include Hushmail, Anonymizer and ZipLip.

Hushmail
http://www.hushmail.com
One of the great new developments on the internet has been dedicated web-based email services like Hotmail, Yahoo! mail, and Excite mail. The advantage is that you can have an international email address that you can access from anywhere in the world without needing your own ISP access. You can use a computer belonging to a friend – or log on at an internet cafe. Now the idea has gone one step further with the introduction of an encrypted web-based email service: HushMail.

Hushmail uses extremely powerful 1024 bit encryption. The log-on process creates your key by taking information from your mouse as you move it around. Your choice of password controls how secure your mailings are. In other words, the more difficult your password is to crack, the more secure your messages.

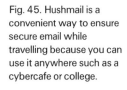

Fig. 45. Hushmail is a convenient way to ensure secure email while travelling because you can use it anywhere such as a cybercafe or college.

HushMail uses Java applets to encrypt your web-based email with public-key encryption. It claims to be the world's first, 'fully encrypted, truly secure, free web-based email client.'

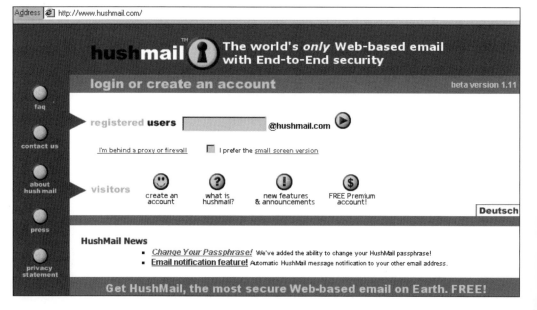

▶ *Email client* – another term used for your email program.

▶ *Web client* – another term used for your web browser.

The main drawback is that the person you're emailing also needs to have a HushMail account in order to decode your message. There are also slight risks from the use of Java and the fact that you have to trust one company – unlike a chain of anonymous remailers. For people who want good security and need the ability to send and receive email from anywhere, such as journalists, HushMail is great.

Signing on to use HushMail is simple – just click on 'Create an Account' and you'll be asked for a username and some other information. Move your mouse around to generate a random set of keys and you're ready to send secure email. You don't need any special software or complicated configuration and registration can be done in less than two minutes.

HushMail uses a process called 'public key cryptosystem with roaming user capability.' That means the only people who can read your mail are the people you send it to. it also means that you can access your account from any computer which has a web browser and internet access, anywhere in the world.

ZipLip
http://www.ZipLip.com
ZipLip is a web-based email service rather similar to HushMail. Your message is stored in encrypted format at the site itself and ZipLip notifies your recipient that your message is waiting for them. In turn, your recipient goes to ZipLip and picks up the message. After it has been read, all traces of the message are removed.

ZipLip uses encryption techniques based on Verisign certificates. However, the problem of exporting encryption products does not arise because the message never leaves their server.

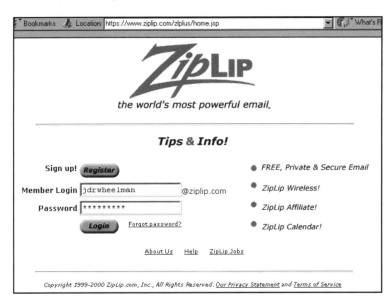

Fig. 46. ZipLip offers another solution for sending and receiving emails very securely.

Email on the move ....

If you protect your mail with a password, your message and the password is stored in an encrypted format that not even ZipLip can read. Your message is decrypted only when the recipient supplies the correct password. There is no registration or information to give away about yourself.

Anonymizer
http://www.anonymizer.com
They say: 'Whether you know it or not, every time you visit a site on the internet you provide information about yourself. You broadcast details about your geographical location, interests, browsing habits, and even the computer you are using to each site you visit and to other entities watching your network. Many web sites and ISPs log this information, compile dossiers on their users, and sell such information to advertisers and marketing firms. The Anonymizer gives you the power to shield your information from prying eyes. It has been the leader in stemming the tide of online privacy invasion since 1996.' The service offers easy-to-use anonymous web surfing, email, web publishing, and secure dial-up services. A very large number of people appear to use it.

Fig. 47. Anonymizer is a well-established and widely used service. It offers a range of anonymity services for internet users.

Using your existing email mailbox

As long as you have an email account through an internet service provider or you sign up for a free POP mail account, you can easily access your existing mailbox from just about any web browser using one of the Web-based POP mail interfaces such as:

Mail2Web
http://www.mail2web.com
http://www.mail2pda.com
http://www.mail2wap.com

Mail2Web enables you to use your POP3 email through an easy web interface. Even if you are travelling around the world, Mail2Web lets you read and reply to your email. You can use Windows, Macintosh or a Unix computer. Mail2Web says that your activities are private and that none of them will be recorded. For really effective security you can use its 128-bit secure service. If you need to access your email from your PDA (personal data assistant) you can use Mail2Web's special PDA facility. If you use your WAP-compatible mobile phone for email, you can use its special WAP facility (see the three web site addresses above). This is how Mail2-Web works. Firstly, the user enters his/her address and password; the Mail2Web server then extracts the POP3 server details from the email address, logs on to the POP3 server where the user account resides and gets the messages in the user's mailbox. Mail2Web formats (and en-crypts) this information and sends it back to the user. Mail2Web says that once the user has finished reading mail and he/she logs off, Mail2-Web forgets that user forever.

Fig. 48. Web2Mail offers web-based email for browsers, PDAs (personal data assistants) and mobile phones via WAP (wireless application protocol).

Acemail
http://www.astray.com/acmemail/

If you were away in Japan for business, you could check your home mail without having to dial your ISP's number, which could cost you rather a lot of money.

Checking your mail server details

To use mail-to-web services, you will need to know your email server name, your username and your password. It's a good idea to test the system from your own home first. Make time to send and retrieve some test emails before you start your journey.

Outlook Express
To find out your details in Outlook Express:

1. Open the Tools menu.

2. Select Accounts.

Email on the move ....

3. Double-click the email account you want to use when you are travelling.

4. Select the Servers tab.

5. Write down the settings in the POP3 Server, SMPT Server, and Account Name boxes.

You should also make sure that you know and can remember your password because you may need this every time you check your mail.

If you want to be able to read the messages in your email mailbox when you get home from your trip, choose to leave them on the server if the site allows this.

Fig. 49. Checking your mail server details in Outlook Express.

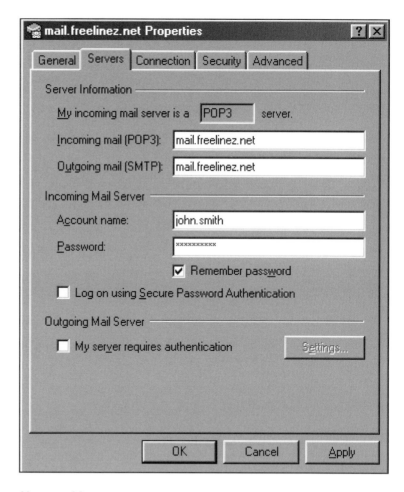

Netscape Messenger
To find out your details in Netscape Messenger:

1. On the main Netscape toolbar click Edit, then Preferences.

2. Click Mail & Newsgroups, then Mail Servers.

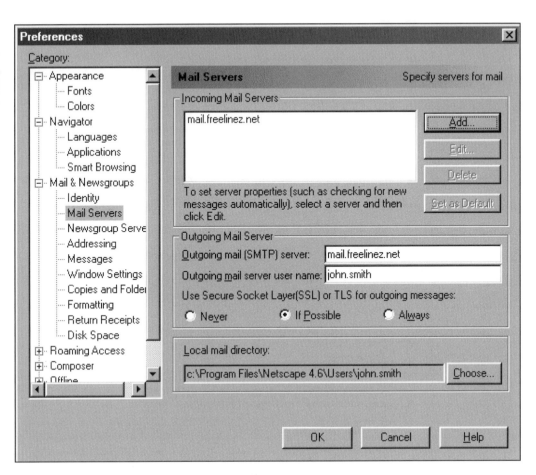

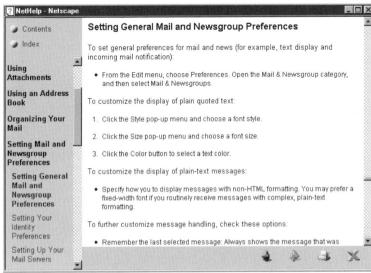

Fig. 50. Checking your mail server details in Netscape Messenger. *Left:* The Messenger Help area is a useful resource.

8 Anything goes

In this chapter we will explore

- ▶ *FTP by email*
- ▶ *Usenet by email*
- ▶ *the world wide web by email*
- ▶ *searching the web by email*
- ▶ *Usenet by email*
- ▶ *reading Usenet newsgroups by email*
- ▶ *posting messages in Usenet newsgroups*
- ▶ *note on Usenet posting*
- ▶ *email to snail mail*
- ▶ *sending a fax by email*
- ▶ *automatic message translation*

. . . .

If you feel that your access to the internet through your ISP or your company is inadequate, don't worry, you can get around the problem by using email.

But if you think that sounds limiting, think again. You can access almost any internet service using email. For example FTP, Usenet and the world wide web are all within reach indirectly via email. You can use simple email commands to access all of these services and many others. And even if you do have full internet access, using email services can save you time and money.

FTP by email

FTP, file transfer protocol, is a way of accessing files that are stored on remote computer systems. It is very like accessing files on your own personal computer using Windows Explorer.

When visiting an FTP site in the normal way, you need to use special software to access that site. You then navigate the directory system of that site in order to find and select one or more files to transfer back to your computer.

Using FTP by email is very similar. The difference is that you work via a special FTPmail server that logs onto the remote site and returns files to you. You send commands to the FTPmail server in the form of an email message.

Receiving files in this way can be better than even with full internet access. This is because many FTP sites are heavily loaded and can run very slowly if you access them directly. With email access, however, the delay can be avoided.

For a comprehensive list of anonymous FTP sites (23 sections), send an email message to:

mail-server@rtfm.mit.edu

Include the following lines of text in the BODY of your note:

    send usenet/news.answers/ftp-list/sitelist/part1
    send usenet/news.answers/ftp-list/sitelist/part2

and so on, until you have listed the final section

    send usenet/news.answers/ftp-list/sitelist/part23

You will then receive 23 messages containing lots of FTP sites and details of the kind of files stored there.

You should also get hold of the 'FTP Frequently Asked Questions'. This very useful item contains lots of information on how to use FTP services. So add this line to your message as well:

    send usenet/news.answers/ftp-list/faq

Retrieving files by email

If you find an interesting FTP site in the list, send an email to one of these FTPmail servers:

ftpmail@academ.com	United States
ftpmail@btoy1.rochester.ny.us	United States
ftpmail@ftp.sunet.se	Sweden
ftpmail@ftp.uni-stuttgart.de	Germany
ftpmail@mercure.umh.ac.be	Belgium

You should be able to use any of these email-to-FTP servers. If one does not work, try another. To use them, send an email with these lines in the body of the message:

    open <site>
    dir
    quit

Your reply may not arrive for several minutes, hours or days, but once it does arrive, you will receive a list of the files stored in the root directory at that site. For example, the following response was received when using the site ftp.simtel.net:

```
total 52328
-rw-rw-r- 1 root wheel        696 Nov 19 1997 README
-rw-rw-r- 1 root wheel       2744 Sep 26 1998 UPLOADS.TXT
drwxrwxr-x 2 root wheel        512 Oct 5 1998 archive-info
lrwxr-xr-x 1 root wheel         21 Nov 22 1998 catalog.txt -> pub/cdrom/catalog.txt
lrwxr-xr-x 1 root wheel         26 Nov 22 1998 config.txt -> archive-info/wcarchive.txt
drwxr-xr-x 2 root wheel        512 May 2 1999 etc
-rw-r—r— 1 root wheel    46696026 May 20 12:26 ls-IR
-rw-r—r— 1 root wheel     6876860 May 20 12:27 ls-IR.gz
drwxrwxr-x 2 root wheel       2048 Mar 3 05:10 pub
```

Anything goes..

You can see the file names on the right preceded by the file size and date. In your next email message you can navigate to other directories by using (for example):

```
open <site>
cd pub          ( if cd doesn't work, use chdir)
dir
```

The 'cd' stands for 'change directory' and 'pub' is usually the public directory on most ftp servers.

Once you find the file you want to retrieve, use:

```
get <name of file>
```

in the body of a message. If the file you want to retrieve is plain text, this will suffice. If it's a binary file (an executable program, compressed file, etc) you'll need to insert the following command before the 'get' command:

```
binary
```

The first file you should download, 'get', is catalog.txt or index.txt or something similar. This will give you a description of the files in the directory.

Large files may be sent to you as multiple messages that your email client will then knit together.

The world wide web by email

It is unfortunate that more and more methods are being introduced to control and limit people's access to the world wide web (WWW). Many employers, for example, do not permit direct access to the web. Back door access to the web is via email. The world wide web is such an important resource that surely no adult internet user should be barred from its free use.

How to use an Agora server
You can retrieve web documents by email by using an 'Agora' server. All you need to know is the address of the web site in question. You can retrieve this by sending email to one of the following servers:

agora@dna.affrc.go.jp

agora@kamakura.mss.co.jp

In the body of your message include the following, replacing 'URL' with the address of the site:

```
send URL
```

for example:

86

send http://www.yahoo.com

If you want the page sent to a different email address, type the following:

rsend return-address URL

for example:

rsend kyevalongo@freeUK.com http://www.yahoo.com

This will send you the web page you requested, with a list of all the other documents that it references. You simply request the other documents as you need them.
Try sending the following commands, for example:

help

send http://www.yahoo.com

After a time, you will receive the Agora help file – essential reading if you plan to browse the web by email – and the start page of Yahoo! directory.
Some other webmail servers are:

getweb@emailfetch.com   use GET URL

getweb@usa.healthnet.org   use GET URL

webmail@www.ucc.ie   use GO URL

There are also some new servers that combine the services of other email-to-web servers and add other features. Send a message with help in the body of the message:

www4mail@ftp.uni-stuttgart.de

www4mail@unganisha.idrc.ca

www4mail@web.bellanet.org

www4mail@wm.ictp.trieste.it

And, for an up-to-date list:

http://www.geocities.com/CapitolHill/1236/servers.html

Searching the web by email

Access to the web is no good unless you can find something of interest. There are several search engines that allow you to search for information on the web, and you don't have to use a web browser to use them. Perhaps the easiest way to access search engines is to send a message

Anything goes...

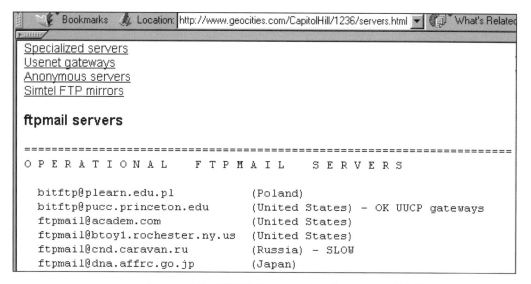

Fig. 51. This web site at Geocities is a useful source of FTPmail servers.

to one of the GETWEB servers (see list on page 87). Type a command in the message body in the following form:

SEARCH YAHOO football

You can also use AltaVista or Infoseek instead of Yahoo! and, of course, your own search words in place of 'football'. Here's an example:

SEARCH YAHOO consumer protection

It is also possible to perform a search indirectly by modifying the URL of a search site, and requesting that URL as you would any other web page. Below are examples for the search engines Lycos and Webcrawler. Just enter the URL, and separate the search keywords with plus signs ('+'). For example:

http://www.lycos.com/srch/?lpv=1&loc=searchhp&query= football+ tickets

http://www.webcrawler.com/cgi-bin/WebQuery?searchText= cat+food

Usenet by email

Established for many years longer than the world wide web, Usenet now contains over 80,000 newsgroups. These range from groups created as a joke to groups used by large groups of professionals. Almost every hobby or interest has one or more newsgroups dedicated to it. Some newsgroups have been dormant for years, but others generate hundreds of new posts ('articles') every day.

The proper and best way to access newsgroups is by using a news client on your computer, such as Outlook Express or Netscape Messenger. Your news client connects to a news server – usually run by your internet service provider – and retrieves messages from whichever groups you decide to subscribe to.

You can also access newsgroups by email, though this can become a tedious process.

Getting a list of newsgroups by email
To get a listing of Usenet newsgroups, send an email message to:

mail-server@rtfm.mit.edu

Place the following commands in the body of your message:

send usenet/news.answers/active-newsgroups/part1
(also get part2 & part3)

send usenet/news.answers/alt-hierarchies/part1
(also get part2 & part3)

Newsgroups FAQs
To get a FAQ (set of Frequently Asked Questions) for a particular news-group, type the following in your message:

index usenet/ < newsgroupname >

Reading Usenet newsgroups by email

Once you've handled the preliminaries, you will need to know how to read and contribute to Usenet newsgroups by email. To read the mes-sages in a newsgroup, you can use a webmail server to retrieve

Fig. 52. Using Deja.com, you can search and read and post messages on thousands of Usenet newsgroups. By email, however, the process can be cumbersome and time-consuming.

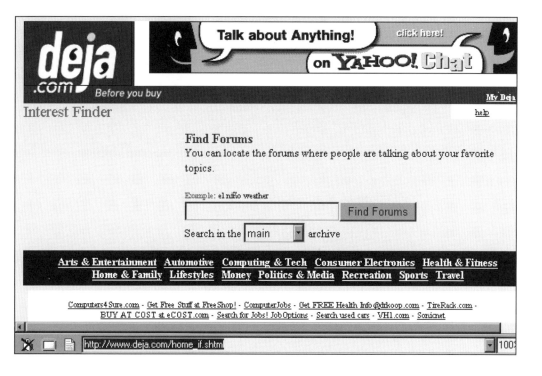

Anything goes..

Deja.com and other web sites that deal with Usenet:

Deja
http://www.deja.com
This very popular service archives all the messages in the Usenet news-groups daily.

Find Forum
http://www.deja.com/home_if.shtml

Browse Group
http://www.deja.com/home_bg.shtml

Power Browse Group
http://www.deja.com/home_ps.shtml

You could also use the Sonador Usenet-by-email server. To get the help file send a blank email to:

autonews_info@sonador.com

Another server is the Relcom Usenet News mailserver. Type the word 'help' in the body of a message and send it to:

newsserv@litech.net

Posting messages in Usenet newsgroups

If you decide to post a message of your own, here are two methods to try. Mail the text of your post to:

group.name@newsgw.rrze.uni-erlangen.de

or mail it to:

mail2news-YYYYMMDD-group.name@anon.lcs.mit.edu

For example, to post to a newsgroup called news.newusers.questions, you might send your message to:

news.newusers.questions@newsgw.rrze.uni-erlangen.de

or you might send it to:

mail2news- 20000512-news.newusers.questions@anon.lcs.mit.edu

Include a subject line, a name and an email address. With the second server, substitute today's date instead of YYMMDD and the newsgroup name instead of 'group.name'. For more information, send a message with 'help' in the subject line to:

mail2news@anon.lcs.mit.edu.

Another web site you might want to look at for more information is:

Replay
http://www.replay.com

Note on Usenet posting

Use your browser or a webmail server to get Don Kitchen's helpful document at:

http://www.sabotage.org/~don/mail2news.html

See page 86 for help with retrieving web pages by email. This document contains tips on finding out whether a mail server supports your newsgroup, how to keep your address away from junk mailers, and an updated list of mail-to-news servers.

Searching for Usenet newsgroups
If you don't know the name of the newsgroup that you are interested in, search for Usenet groups about your subject by accessing the Alabanza web site (using the method on page 86 if you only have email access to the web). Use the following URL with the keyword added onto the end:

http:// alabanza.com

For example, to search for groups concerned with football, use:

http://alabanza.com/kabacoff/Inter-Links/cgi/news.cgi?football

Email to snail mail

If the person you want to contact doesn't have email, you can send it to an 'email to snail mail' service. They will print your message on a quality printer, envelope it, and post it to the address you specify. There is a charge for the service, but it is small compared with the cost of sending a telegram.

PaperMail
A UK-based service called PaperMail charges £1 for each letter sent in this way. You pay an initial deposit of £25 and the cost of each letter sent is deducted from this. You can top up the deposit at any time so you can carry on sending letters. If you send PaperMail a supply of your own stationery, they will use it for your letters at no extra cost.

They say: 'It should arrive the next day in Britain, and within a few days anywhere in North-West Europe – almost certainly quicker than if you posted it from outside Europe.'

For full details on PaperMail and other services in other countries, send a blank email to:

info@papermail.win-uk.net

Anything goes...

The Phone Company's Remote Printing Service

TPC FAX

Welcome to the TPC home page. The TPC service is a collection of FAX servers you may use to send a fax by e-mail to many locations around the world.

Several sites are available in various parts of the internet that maintain complete mirrors of the TPC.INT site. **Please select a mirror closest to you.**

- **Canada Mirror** (Toronto)

- **Canada Mirror** (New Brunswick)

- **Croatian Mirror**

- **Germany Mirror**

- **Italy Mirror**

- **Russia Mirror** (Moscow) in Russian (out of date)

- **United Kingdom Mirror**

Fig. 53. The Phone Company (TPC) service is a collection of FAX servers that you can use to send a fax by email to many places around the world.

Sending a fax by email

TPC
http://www.tpc.int/
Converting an email message to fax is easy. The TPC.INT remote printing experiment was perhaps the first internet faxing service. For full information about TPC's service , send email to them at:

> tpcfaq@info.tpc.int

Do not put a subject line, but put the word 'help' in the body of the message. For a list of countries served by this service, send email to them at:

> tpccover@info.tpc.int

with no subject and nothing in the body.
   Or you can go to the web site (or retrieve by email) for free service to some areas.

More fax information and possibilities
Alternatively you can visit JFax, which charges a fee for its world wide service:

> http://www.jfax.com/

You can also get the FAX FAQ via electronic mail. Send email to:

> mail-server@rtfm.mit.edu

and enter only this line in the body of the note:

    send usenet/news.answers/internet-services/fax-faq

Another FAQ is available from:

    http://www.savetz.com/fax/

For other things you can do with email, send blank email to:

    email4u@wireworm.com

For more details on using web search engines by email use a web-to-mail server to get this file:

    send ftp://ftp.netcom.com/pub/gb/gboyd/wsintro.faq

Automatic message translation

It is now possible to send an email to a colleague in another country and have it translated.

T-Mail
http://www.t-mail.com/index2.shtml
This is perhaps the best translation service currently available on the internet. Send a message as normal but type in the appropriate T-Mail address in the 'Cc:' line of the message before you send it. When T-Mail receives the 'Cc:', it translates the email message from one language to another. The original message is delivered as usual to the person on the 'To:' line and the copy is translated and also sent to the same person.

Fig. 54. The universal translator of Star Trek is a step closer to reality with the great work that is being done by T-Mail. This neat language translator can cope with English, French, German and other languages, if not yet Klingon!

Anything goes..

If, for example you need to send a message to confirm a hire car with a German hotel, you can send the message:

To: hiltonhotel@frankfurt.de
Cc: English-German@T-Mail.com
Subject: Car hire confirmation
Please confirm the availability of a car for Mr. Valongo on the 12th December 2000.

Make sure that the message is text only, and that it contains no attachments. The hotel will receive the original message. The second message, which was sent via the 'Cc:' instructions to T-Mail, is translated from English into German and forwarded on. In this case, the translation was:

Bestätigen Sie bitte die Verfügbarkeit eines Autos für Herrn Valongo am 12 Dezember 2000.

The hotel gets two messages – the original in English and the translation from T-mail. For other languages format the 'Cc:' like this:

(Original language) - (Final translation)@T-Mail.com

Using the following language codes:

1. English or en
2. French or fr
3. German or ge or de
4. Italian or it
5. Spanish or sp or es
6. Portuguese or pt or po

A Portuguese to French translation would be:

Portuguese-French@t-mail.com

or:

pt-fr@t-mail.com

or:

po-fr@t-mail.com

For information on which languages are currently translated, look at T-Mail's main web page:

T-Mail
http://www.T-Mail.com.

Appendix 1: Essential websites

. . . .

History of the internet

The History of the Internet
http://www.pbs.org/internet/timeline/

A Short History of the Internet
http://info.isoc.org/guest/zakon/Internet/History/Short_History_of_
the_Internet

Getting connected

Directory of Free ISPs
http://www.a2zweblinks.com/freeukisp/index.htm

Macintosh: Open Transport Help
http://www2.netdoor.com/~rreid/opentransport/

Windows: How to Set Up A Winsock Connection – A Beginner's Guide
http://omni.cc.purdue.edu/~xniu/winsock.htm

The world wide web

Newbie U's Web Stadium
http://www.newbie-u.com/web/

All About the World Wide Web
http://www.imaginarylandscape.com/helpweb/www/www.html

Sink or Swim: Internet Search Tools & Techniques
http://www.ouc.bc.ca/libr/connect96/search.htm

Search Engine Shoot-out: Search Engines Compared
http://www.cnet.com/Content/Reviews/Compare/Search2/

Email

Everything E-mail
http://everythingemail.net/

A Beginner's Guide to Effective Email
http://www.webfoot.com/advice/email.top.html

How to find people's E-mail addresses
http://www.qucis.queensu.ca/FAQs/email/finding.html

Discussion forums

E-Mail Discussion Groups/Lists Resources
http://www.webcom.com/impulse/list.html

Appendix: Essential websites...

The List of Lists
http://catalog.com/vivian/interest-group-search.html

FTP

Anonymous FTP FAQ
http://www.cis.ohio-state.edu/hypertext/faq/usenet/ftp-list/faq/faq.html

Multimedia File Formats on the Internet
http://www.lib.rochester.edu/multimed/intro.htm
Covers downloading files, file formats, ways to use the files, and ftp software.

Privacy and security on the internet

Electronic Privacy Information Centre (EPIC)
http://www.epic.org
EPIC is a research centre in Washington. It was established in 1994 to focus public attention on civil liberties issues and to protect privacy, the First Amendment, and constitutional values. EPIC works in association with the London human rights group Privacy International.

Internet Freedom
http://www.netfreedom.org
Internet Freedom is opposed to all forms of censorship and content regulation on the Net. The site mainly consists of news about the many forms of censorship.

Privacy International
http://www.privacyinternational.org
Their site says, 'Privacy International is a human rights group formed in 1990 as a watchdog on surveillance by governments and corporations. PI is based in London, and has an office in Washington, D.C. PI has conducted campaigns in Europe, Asia and North America to counter abuses of privacy by way of information technology such as telephone tapping, ID card systems, video surveillance, data matching, police information systems, and medical records.'

Privacy Rights Clearing House
http://www.privacyrights.org
The PRC provides in-depth information on a variety of informational privacy issues, as well as tips on safeguarding your personal privacy. The PRC was established with funding from the Telecommunications Education Trust, a program of the California Public Utilities Commission.

Appendix 2: Manually configuring your software

Some installation CDs supplied by ISPs can play havoc with your computer setup. You may therefore want to be able to bypass the automatic installation and do it manually. To do this, you need four pieces of information:

1. The dial up telephone number of your ISP.

2. Your exact email address with your new ISP.

3. The name of your incoming mail server (POP3 or IMAP), e.g. mail.virgin.net (if your ISP is Virgin Net).

4. The name of your outgoing mail (SMTP) server, e.g. mail.virgin.net (if your ISP is Virgin Net).

Setting up a new Dial-Up Networking entry

1. Select Dial-Up Networking from within the My Computer icon on the desktop, or you can click on Start, Programs, Accessories then Communications (if you have Windows 98).

2. Double-click the icon labelled Make New Connection.

3. Enter any name you like to describe the connection.

4. Click Next.

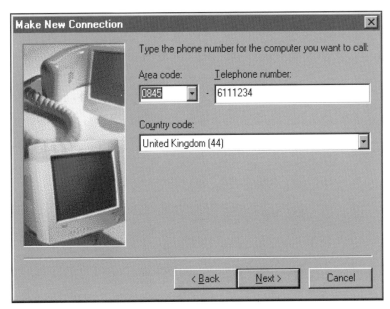

Fig. 55. Setting up a new Dial-Up Networking entry.

Manually configuring your software ....

5. Enter the area code, usually 0845, followed by the dial-up telephone number of your ISP.

6. Click Next, then Finish.

Setting Up Outlook Express

If you want to add a new email account to Outlook Express:

1. Click on Tools, then Accounts.

2. Click on the Add button and select Mail.

3. Type your full email address in the box, and then click Next.

4. Type in the name of the Incoming Mail (POP3 or IMAP) Server, e.g. mail.virgin.net (if your ISP is Virgin Net).

5. Type in the name of the Outgoing mail (SMTP) Server, e.g. mail.virgin.net (if your ISP is Virgin Net).

6. Click Next.

7. Enter your email username and password in the boxes, and then click Next.

8. Finally, choose a descriptive name for your mail account.

9. Click Next to continue.

Fig. 56. Adding a new email account to Outlook Express.

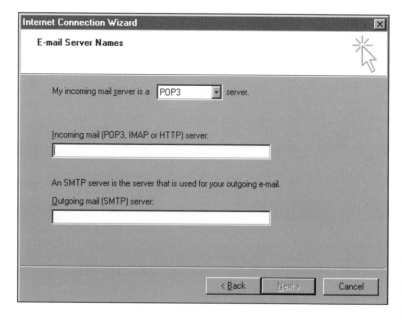

98

10. If you use a modem to connect to the internet, select 'Connect using my phone line', then click Next.

11. Select the dial-up connection that you want to use and click Next.

12. Click Finish.

Netscape Messenger

To manually set up Netscape Communicator:

1. Click on Edit, and then Preferences.

2. Click on the Mail Servers tab, and then on Add.

3. Enter the server name, e.g. mail.virgin.net (if your ISP is Virgin Net).

4. Enter your user name.

5. When you click on OK this will take you to the main screen. Here, you should enter the name of the outgoing mail server in the Outgoing Mail (SMTP) Server field, e.g. mail.virgin.net (if your ISP is Virgin Net).

6. When you want to connect to the internet, select Dial-Up Networking from your My Computer, or click Start, Programs, Accessories then Communications (if you have Windows 98). Double-click on the DUN entry you wish to use.

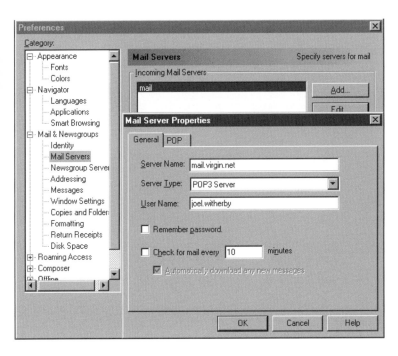

Fig. 57. Setting up your mail server and user name using Netscape Messenger.

Glossary of internet terms

Access provider – The company that provides you with access to the internet. This may be an independent provider or a large international organisation such as AOL or CompuServe. See also **internet service provider**.

ActiveX – A Microsoft programming language that allows effects such as animations, games and other interactive features to be included a web page.

Adobe Acrobat – A type of software required for reading PDF files ('portable document format'). You may need to have Adobe Acrobat Reader when downloading large text files from the internet, such as lengthy reports or chapters from books. If your computer lacks it, the web page will prompt you, and usually offer you an immediate download of the free version.

address book – A directory in a web browser where you can store people's email addresses. This saves having to type them out each time you want to email someone. You just click on an address whenever you want it.

ADSL – Asymmetric Digital Subscriber Line, a new phone line technology which provides an internet connexion speed up to 10 times faster than a typical modem.

Adult check – An age verification system that only allows the over 18s to enter adult web sites.

affiliate programme – A system that allows you to sell other companies products via your web site.

age verification service (AVS) – A commercial system that prevent minors from accessing adult oriented web sites.

AltaVista – One of the half dozen most popular internet search engines. Just type in a few key words to find what you want on the internet. See: www.altavista.com

AOL – America On Line, the world's biggest internet service provider, with more than 25 million subscribers, and now merged with Time Warner. Because it has masses of content of its own - quite aside from the wider internet - it is sometimes referred to as an 'online' service provider rather than internet service provider. It has given away vast numbers of free CDs with the popular computer magazines to build its customer base. It also owns Netscape. See: www.aol.com

Apple Macintosh – A type of computer that has its own proprietary operating system, as distinct from the MSDOS and Windows operating systems found on PCs (personal computers). The Apple Mac has long been a favourite of designers and publishers.

applet – An application programmed in Java that is designed to run only on a web browser. Applets cannot read or write data onto your computer, only from the domain in which they are served from. When a web page using an applet is accessed, the browser will download it and run it on your computer. See also **Java**.

application – Any program, such as a word processor or spreadsheet program, designed to carry out a task on your computer.

application service provider – A company that provides computer software via the internet, whereby the application is borrowed, rather than downloaded. You keep your data, they keep the program.

ARPANET – Advanced Research Projects Agency Network, an early form of the internet in the USA in the 1960s.

ASCII – American Standard Code for Information Interchange. It is a simple text file format that can be accessed by most word processors and text editors. It is a universal file type for passing textual information across the internet.

Ask Jeeves – A popular internet search engine. Rather than just typing in a few key words for your search, you can type in a whole question or instruction, such as 'Find me everything about online investment.' It draws on a database of millions of questions and answers, and works best with fairly general questions.

ASP – (1) Active Server Page, a filename extension for a type of web page. (2) Application service provider (see above).

attachment – A file sent with an email message. The attached file can be anything from a word-processed document to a database, spreadsheet, graphic, or even a sound or video file. For example you could email someone birthday greetings, and attach a sound track or video clip.

Authenticode – Authenticode is a system where ActiveX controls can be authenticated in some way, usually by a certificate.

avatar – A cartoon or image used to represent someone on screen while taking part in internet chat.

AVS – Age verification system, a system that only allows the over 18s to enter adult web sites.

backup – A second copy of a file or a set of files. Backing up data is essential if there is any risk of data loss.

bandwidth – The width of the electronic highway that gives you access to the internet. The higher the bandwidth, the wider this highway, and the faster the traffic can flow.

banner ad – This is a band of text and graphics, usually situated at the top of a web page. It acts like a title, telling the user what the content of the page is about. It invites the visitor to click on it to visit that site. Banner advertising has become big business.

baud rate – The data transmission speed in a modem, measured in bps (bits per second).

BBS – Bulletin board service. A facility to read and to post public messages at a particular web site.

binary numbers – The numbering system used by computers. It only uses 1s and 0s to represent numbers. Decimal numbers are based on the number 10. You can count from nought to nine. When you count higher than nine, the nine is replaced with a 10. Binary numbers are based on the number 2: each place can only have the value of 1 or 0.

Blue Ribbon Campaign – A widely supported campaign supporting free speech and opposing moves to censor the internet by all kinds of elected and unelected bodies. See the Electronic Frontier Foundation at: www.eff.org

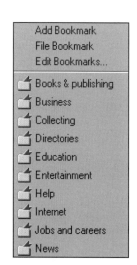

bookmark – A file of URLs of your favourite internet sites. – Bookmarks are very easily created by bookmarking (mouse-clicking) any internet page you like the look of. If you are an avid user, you could soon end up with hundreds of them! In the Internet Explorer browser and AOL they are called Favorites.

Boolean search – A search in which you type in words such as AND and OR to refine your search. Such words are called 'Boolean operators'. The concept is named after George Boole, a nineteenth-century English mathematician.

bot – Short for robot. It is used to refer to a program that will perform a task on the internet, such as carrying out a search.

browser – Your browser is your window to the internet, and will normally supplied by your internet service provider when you first sign up. It is the program that you use to access the world wide web, and manage your personal communications and privacy when online. By far the two most popular browsers are Microsoft Internet Explorer and Netscape Communicator. You can easily swap, or use both. Both can be downloaded free from their web sites (a lengthy process) and are found on the CD roms stuck to the computer magazines. It won't make much difference which one you use - they both do much the same thing. Opera (www.opera.com) is an alternative, as is Net-

Captor (www.netcaptor.com). America Online (www.aol.com) has its own proprietary browser which is not available separately.

bug – A weakness in a program or a computer system. They are remedied by 'fixes' which can be downloaded.

bulletin board – A type of computer-based news service that provides an email service and a file archive.

cache – A file storage area on a computer. Your web browser will normally cache (copy to your hard drive) each web page you visit. When you revisit that page on the web, you may in fact be looking at the page originally cached on your computer. To be sure you are viewing the current page, press **reload** or **refresh** on your browser toolbar. You can empty your cache from time to time, and the computer will do so automatically whenever the cache is full. In Internet Explorer, pages are saved in the Windows folder, Temporary Internet Files. In Netscape they are saved in a folder called Cache.

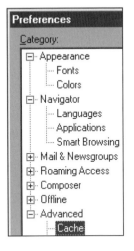

certificate – A computer file that securely identifies a person or organisation on the internet.

CGI – Common gateway interface. This defines how the web server should pass information to the program, such as what it's being asked to do, what objects it should work with, any inputs, and so on. It is the same for all web servers.

channel (chat) – Place where you can chat with other internet chatters. The name of a chat channel is prefixed with a hash mark, #.

clickstream – The sequence of hyperlinks clicked by someone when using the internet.

click through – This is when someone clicks on a banner ad or other link, for example, and is moved from that page to the advertiser's web site.

client – This is the term given to any program that you use to access the internet. For example your web browser is a web client, your email program is an email client, your newsreader is a news client, and your chat software is a chat client.

co-locating – Putting your computer at another company's location so you can connect your web site permanently to the internet.

community – The internet is often described as a net community. This refers to the fact that many people like the feeling of belonging to a group of like-minded individuals. Many big web sites have been developed along these lines, such as GeoCities (www.geocities.com) which is divided into special-interest neighbourhoods, or America Online (www.aol.com) which is strong on member services.

compression – Computer files can be electronically compressed, so that they can be uploaded or downloaded more quickly across the internet, saving time and money. If an image file is compressed too much, there may be a loss of quality. To read them, you uncompress – 'unzip' – them.

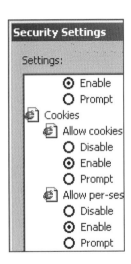

configure – To set up, or adjust the settings of, a computer or software program.

content – The articles, messages, forums, images, text, hyperlinks and other features of a web site.

cookie – A cookie is a small text file that the server asks your browser to keep until it asks for it. If it sends it with the first page and asks for it back before each other page, they can follow you around the site, even if you switch your computer off in between.

cracker – Someone who breaks into computer systems with the intention of causing some kind of damage or system abuse.

crash – What happens when a computer program malfunctions. The operating system of your PC may perform incorrectly or come to a complete stop ('freeze'), forcing you to shut down and restart.

cross-posting – Posting an identical message in several different newsgroups at the same time.

cybercash – This is a trademark, but is also often used as a broad term to describe the use of small payments made over the internet using a new form of electronic account that is loaded up with cash. You can send this money to the companies offering such cash facilities by cheque, or by credit card. Some internet companies offering travel-related items can accept electronic cash of this kind.

cyberspace – Popular term for the intangible 'place' where you go to surf - the ethereal and borderless world of computers and telecommunications on the internet.

cypherpunk – From the cypherpunk mailing list charter: 'Cypherpunks assume privacy is a good thing and wish there were more of it. Cypherpunks acknowledge that those who want privacy must create it for themselves and not expect governments, corporations, or other large, faceless organisations to grant them privacy out of beneficence.'

cypherpunk remailer – Cypherpunk remailers strip headers from the messages and add new ones.

cybersquatting – Using someone else's name or trademark as your domain name in the hope they will buy it from you.

cyberstalker – An individual who pursues someone using online methods such as email, chat rooms and newsgroups.

data – Pieces of information (singular: datum). Data can exist in many forms such as numbers in a spreadsheet, text in a document, or as binary numbers stored in a computer's memory.

database – A store of information in digital form. Many web sites make use of substantial databases to deliver maximum content at high speed to the web user.

dial-up account – This allows you to connect your (local) computer to your internet service provider's (remote) computer.

digital – Based on the two binary digits, 1 and 0. The operation of all computers is based on this amazingly simple concept. All forms of information are capable of being digitalised - numbers, words, and even sounds and images - and then transmitted over the internet.

digital signature – A unique and secure personal signature specially created for use over the internet. It is designed to fulfil a similar function to that of the traditional handwritten signature.

directory – On a PC, a folder containing your files.

DNS – Domain name server.

domain name – A name that identifies an IP address. It identifies to the computers on the rest of the internet where to access particular information. Each domain has a name. For someone@somewhere.co.uk, 'somewhere' is the domain name.

download – Downloading means copying a file from one computer on the internet to your own computer. You do this by clicking on a button that links you to the appropriate file. Downloading is an automatic process, except that you have to click 'yes' to accept the download and give it a file name. You can download any type of file - text, graphics, sound, spreadsheet, computer programs, and so on.

ebusiness The broad concept of doing business to business, and business to consumer sales, over the internet.

ecash – Short for electronic cash. See cybercash.

Echelon – The name of a massive governmental surveillance facility based in Yorkshire, UK. Operated clandestinely by the USA, UK and certain other governments, it is said to be eavesdropping virtually the entire traffic of the internet. It is said to use special electronic dictionaries to trawl through millions of emails and other transmissions.

ecommerce The various means and techniques of transacting business online.

Dial-Up
Networking

email – Electronic mail, any message or file you send from your computer to another computer using your email client program (such as Netscape Messenger or Microsoft Outlook).

email address – The unique address given to you by your ISP. It can be used by others using the internet to send email messages to you. An email address always has at 'at' sign in the middle, for example:

myname@myISP.com

email bomb – An attack by email where you are sent hundreds or thousands of email messages in a very short period of time. Such an attack could prevent you from receiving genuine email messages.

emoticons – Popular symbols used to express emotions in email, for example the well known smiley

:-)

which means 'I'm smiling!' Emoticons are not normally appropriate for business communications.

encryption – The scrambling of information to make it unreadable without a key or password. Email and any other data can now be encrypted using PGP and other freely available programs. Modern encryption has become so amazingly powerful as to be to all intents and purposes uncrackable. Many governments (including the UK) have responded with draconian surveillance of internet traffic.

Excite – A popular internet directory and search engine used to find pages relating to specific keywords which you enter. See: www.excite.com

ezines – The term for magazines and newsletters published on the internet.

FAQs – Frequently asked questions. You will see 'FAQ' everywhere you go on the internet. If you are ever doubtful about anything check the FAQ page, if the site has one, and you should find the answers to your queries.

favorites – The rather coy term for **bookmarks** used by Internet Explorer, and by America Online. Maintaining a list of Favorites is designed to make returning to web sites easier, by saving their addresses.

file – A file is any body of data such as a word processed document, a spreadsheet, a database file, a graphics or video file, sound file, or computer program. On a PC, every file has a filename, and a filename extension showing what type of file it is.

filtering software – Software loaded onto a computer to prevent access by someone to unwelcome content on the internet, notably porn. The well-known 'parental controls' include CyberSitter, CyberPatrol, SurfWatch and NetNanny. They can be blunt instruments. For example, if they are programmed to reject all web pages containing the word 'virgin', you would not be able to access any web page hosted at Richard Branson's Virgin Net! Of course, there are also web sites that tell you step-by-step how to disable or bypass these filtering tools, notably: www.peacefire.org

finger – A tool for locating people on the internet. The most common use is to see if a person has an account at a particular internet site. It also means a chat command that returns information about the other chat user, including idle time (time since they last did anything).

firewall – A firewall is special security software designed to stop the flow of certain files into and out of a computer network, e.g. viruses or attacks by hackers. A firewall would be an important feature of any fully commercial web site.

flame – A more or less hostile or aggressive message posted in a newsgroup or to an individual newsgroup user. If they get out of hand there can be flame wars.

folder – The name for a directory on a computer. It is a place in which files are

Get Excite

Message Centre

✉ **Your Free Email**

· **Free Voicemail/Fax**

Featured Today

✗ **NEWS:** British barricade a
at N.Irish hotspot

Poll: Summer Film Favour

New! Top Mp3 Downloads

[Chat & Make Friends]

Address ☐ C:\WINDOWS

Folders

Desktop

My Computer

3½ Floppy (A:)

Harddisk_1 (C:)

~mssetup.t

Acrobat3

AOL 5.0

ati

ichat

Inetpub

Info

Infont

Install

Internet Explor

Glossary of internet terms ....

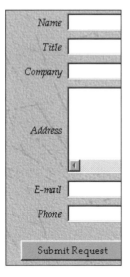

- Top of Report
- General Statistics
- Most Requested Page
- Most Submitted Form
- Most Active Organizations
- Summary of Activity b Day
- Activity Level by Day Week
- Activity Level by Hou
- Technical Statistics

stored.

form – A web page that allows or requires you to enter information into fields on the page and send the information to a web site, program or individual on the web. Forms are often used for registration or sending questions and comments to web sites.

forums – Places for discussion on the internet. They include Usenet newsgroups, mailing lists, and bulletin board services.

frames – A web design feature in which web pages are divided into several areas or panels, each containing separate information. A typical set of frames in a page includes an index frame (with navigation links), a banner frame (for a heading), and a body frame (for text matter).

freebies – The 'give away' products, services or other enticements offered on a web site to attract registrations.

freespace – An allocation of free web space by an internet service provider or other organisation, to its users or subscribers, typically between 5 and 20 megabytes.

freeware – Software programs made available without charge. Where a small charge is requested, the term is **shareware**.

front page – The first page of your web site that the visitor will see. FrontPage is also the name of a popular web authoring package from Microsoft.

FTP – File transfer protocol, the method the internet uses to speed files back and forth between computers. Your browser will automatically select this method, for instance, when you want to download your bank statements to reconcile your accounts. In practice you don't need to worry about FTP unless you are thinking about creating and publishing your own web pages: then you would need some of the freely available FTP software. Despite the name, it's easy to use.

GIF – Graphic interchange format. It is a widely used compressed file format used on web pages and elsewhere to display files that contain graphic images. See also **JPEG**.

GUI – Short for graphic user interface. It describes the user-friendly screens found in Windows and other WIMP environments (windows, icons, mice, pointers).

hacker – A person interested in computer programming, operating systems, the internet and computer security. The term can be used to describe a person who breaks into computer systems with the intention of pointing out the weaknesses in a system. In common usage, the term is often wrongly used to describe crackers.

header – That part of an email message or newsgroup posting which contains information about the sender and the route that the message took across the internet.

history list – A record of visited web pages. Your browser probably includes a history list. It is handy way of revisiting sites whose addresses you have forgotten to bookmark - just click on the item you want in the history list. You can normally delete all or part of the history list in your browser. However, your ISP may well be analysing this information even if you delete it on your own computer (see **internet service providers**, above).

hit counter – A piece of software used by a web site to publicly display the number of hits it has received.

hits – The number of times pieces of text, images, hyperlinks and other components of a web page have been viewed. A better measure of a site's popularity would be the number of page views, or the number of user sessions.

home page – This refers to the index page of an individual or an organisation on the internet. It usually contains links to related pages of information, and to other relevant sites

host – A host is the computer where a particular file or domain is located, and from where people can retrieve it.

HotBot – A popular internet search engine used to find pages relating to any key-words you decide to enter.

HTML – Hyper text markup language, the universal computer language used to create pages on the world wide web. It is much like word processing, but uses special 'tags' for formatting the text and creating hyperlinks to other web pages.

HTTP – Hypertext transfer protocol, the protocol used by the world wide web. It is the language spoken between your browser and the web servers. It is the standard way that HTML documents are transferred from host computer to your local browser when you're surfing the internet. You'll see this acronym at the start of every web address, for example:

http://www.abcxyz.com

With modern browsers, it is no longer necessary to enter 'http://' at the start of the address.

hyperlink – See **link**.

hypertext – This is a link on an HTML page that, when clicked with a mouse, results in a further HTML page or graphic being loaded into view on your browser.

IANA – The Internet Assigned Numbers Authority, the official body responsible for ensuring that the numerical coding of the internet works properly.

ICANN – The committee that oversees the whole domain name system.

ICQ – A form of internet chat, derived from the phrase 'I seek you'. It enables users to be alerted whenever fellow users go online, so they can have instant chat communication. The proprietary software is owned by America Online.

IMAP – Stands for internet messaging access protocol. It is a standard type of mail server that stores incoming emails until users log on and download them. Both IMAP and POP accept SMTP-formatted messages sent over the internet.

impression – An internet advertising term that means the showing of a single instance of an advert on a single computer screen.

Infoseek – One of the ten most popular internet search engines, now teamed up with Disney in the GO Network.

Intel – Manufacturer of the Pentium and Celeron microprocessors.

internet – The broad term for the fast-expanding network of global computers that can access each other in seconds by phone and satellite links. If you are using a modem on your computer, you too are part of the internet. The general term 'internet' encompasses email, the world wide web, internet chat, Usenet newsgroups, mailing lists, bulletin boards, telnet, and video conferencing. It is rather like the way we speak of 'the printed word' when we mean books, magazines, newspapers, newsletters, catalogues, leaflets, tickets and posters. The 'internet' does not exist in one place any more than 'the printed word' does.

Internet2 – A new form of the internet being developed exclusively for educational and academic use.

internet account – The account set up by your internet service provider which gives you access to the world wide web, electronic mail facilities, newsgroups and other value added services.

internet directory – A special web site which consists of information about other sites. The information is classified by subject area and further subdivided into smaller categories. The biggest and most widely used is Yahoo! – www.yahoo.com – See also **search engines**.

Internet Explorer – The world's most popular browser software, a product of Microsoft and leading the field against Netscape.

internet keywords – A commercial service that allows people to find your domain name without having to type in www or .com

Internet protocol number – The numerical code that is a web site's real domain name address, rather than its alphabetical name.

internet service providers – ISPs are commercial, educational or official organisations which offer people ('users') access to the internet. The well-known commercial ones include AOL, CompuServe, BT Internet, Freeserve, Demon and Virgin Net. Services typically include access to the world wide web, email and newsgroups, as well as others such as news, chat, and entertainment. Your internet service provider is able to know everything you do on the internet, involving challenging new issues of personal privacy and data protection.

intranet – A private computer network that uses internet technology to allow communication between individuals, for example within a large commercial organisation. – It often operates on a LAN (local area network).

IP address – An 'internet protocol' address. – All computers linked to the internet have one. The address is somewhat like a telephone number, and consists of four sets of numbers separated by dots.

IPv6 – The new internet coding system that will allow even more domain names.

IRC – Internet relay chat. Chat is an enormously popular part of the internet, and there are all kinds of chat rooms and chat software. The chat involves typing messages which are sent and read in real time. It was developed in 1988 by a Finn called Jarkko Oikarinen.

ISDN – Integrated Services Digital Network. This is a high-speed telephone network that can send computer data from the internet to your PC faster than a normal telephone line.

Java – A programming language developed by Sun Microsystems to use the special properties of the internet to create graphics and multimedia applications on web sites.

JavaScript – A simple programming language that can be put onto a web page to create interactive effects such as buttons that change appearance when you position the mouse over them.

JPEG – The acronym is short for Joint Photographic Experts Group. A JPEG is a specialised file format used to display graphic files on the internet. JPEG files can be smaller than similar GIF files and so have become ever more popular - even though there is sometimes a feeling that their quality is not as good as GIF format files. See also MPEG.

key shortcut – Two keys pressed at the same time. Usually the Control key (Ctrl), Alt key, or Shift key combined with a letter or number. For example, to use Control-D, press Control, tap the D key once firmly, then take your finger off the Control key.

keywords – Words that sum up your web site for being indexed in search engines. For example for a cosmetic site the key words might include beauty, lipstick, make-up, fashion, cosmetic and so on.

kick – To eject someone from a chat channel.

LAN – A local area network, a computer network usually located in one building or campus.

link – A hypertext phrase or image that calls up another web page when you click on it. Most web sites have lots of hyperlinks - links for short. These appear on the screen as buttons, images or bits of text (often underlined) that you can click on with your mouse to jump to another site on the world wide web.

Linux – A new widely and freely available operating system for personal computers, and a potentially serious challenger to Microsoft. It has developed a considerable following.

LINX – The London Internet Exchange, the facility which maintains UK internet

traffic in the UK. It allows existing individual internet service providers to exchange traffic within the UK, and improve connectivity and service for their customers. LINX is one of the largest and fastest growing exchange points in Europe, and maintains connectivity between the UK and the rest of the world.

listserver – An automated email system whereby subscribers are able to receive and send email from other subscribers to the same mailing list. See: www.liszt.com

log on/log off – To access/leave a network. In the early days of computing this literally involved writing a record in a log book. You may be asked to 'log on' to certain sites and particular pages. This normally means entering your user ID in the form of a name and a password.

lurk – The term used to describe reading the messages in a newsgroup without actually posting messages yourself.

macros – 'Macro languages' are used to automate repetitive tasks in Word processors and other applications. They can carry viruses.

mail server – A remote computer that enables you to send and receive emails. Your internet access provider will usually act as your mail server, storing your incoming messages until you go online to retrieve them.

mailing list – A forum where messages are distributed by email to the members of the forum. The two types of lists are discussion and announcement. Discussion lists allow exchange between list members. Announcement lists are one-way only and used to distribute information such as news or humour. A good place to find mailing lists is Liszt : www.liszt.com

marquee – A moving (scrolling) line of text on a web site, normally used for eye-catching purposes.

Media Player – Windows software on a personal computer that will play sounds and images including video clips and animations.

metasearch engine – A site that sends a keyword search to many different search engines and directories so you can use many search engines from one place.

meta tags – The technical term for the keywords used in web page code to help search engine software rank the site.

Microsoft – The world's biggest producer of software for personal computers, including the Windows operating systems, and the web browser Internet Explorer.

MIME – Stands for multipurpose internet mail extensions. It refers to the attachment of non-text files to normal text-based email messages. Such files might include images, sound tracks, spreadsheets, formatted documents and so on. An email program is 'MIME compliant' if it is capable of receiving and sending files using the MIME standard.

mixmaster – A type of anonymous remailer that sends and receives email messages as packages of exactly the same size, and often randomly varies the delay time between receiving and remailing to make interception harder.

modem – This is an internal or external piece of hardware plugged into your PC. It links into a standard phone socket, thereby giving you access to the internet. The word derives from MOdulator and DEModulator.

moderator – A person in charge of a mailing list, newsgroup or forum. The moderator prevents unwanted messages.

MPEG or **MPG** – The file format used for video clips available on the internet. See also JPEG.

MP3 – An immensely popular audio format that allows you to download and play music on your computer. It compresses music to create files that are small yet whose quality is almost as good as CD music. At the time of writing, MP4, even faster to download was being developed. See the consumer web site:

Glossary of internet terms ....

www.mp3.com

MUDs – Multi-user dungeons, interactive chat-based fantasy world games. Popular in the early days of the internet, they are now in decline with the advance of networked action games such as Quake and Unreal.

navigate – To click on the hyperlinks on a web site in order to move to other web pages or internet sites.

net – A slang term for the internet. In the same way, the world wide web is often just called the web.

netiquette – Popular term for the unofficial rules and language people follow to keep electronic communication in an acceptably polite form.

Netmeeting – This Microsoft plug in allows a moving video picture to be contained within a web page. It is now integrated into Windows Media Player.

Netscape – After Microsoft's Internet Explorer, Netscape is the most popular browser software available for surfing the internet. An excellent product, Netscape has suffered in the wake of Internet Explorer, mainly because of the success of Microsoft in getting the latter pre-loaded on most new PCs. Netscape Communicator comes complete with email, newsgroups, address book and bookmarks, plus a web page composer. Netscape is now part of American Online.

nettie – Slang term for someone who likes to spend a lot of time on the internet.

newbie – Popular term for a new member of a newsgroup or mailing list.

newsgroup – A Usenet discussion group. Each newsgroup is a collection of messages, usually unedited and not checked by anyone ('unmoderated'). Anyone can post messages to a newsgroup. It is rather like reading and sending public emails. The ever-growing newsgroups have been around for much longer than the world wide web, and are an endless source of information, gossip, news, entertainment, sex, scandal, politics, resources and ideas. The 80,000-plus newsgroups are collectively referred to as Usenet, and millions of people use it every day.

newsreader – A type of software that enables you to search, read, post and manage messages in a newsgroup. It will normally be supplied by your internet service provider when you first sign up, or preloaded on your new computer. The best known newsreaders are Microsoft Outlook, and Netscape Messenger.

news server – A remote computer (e.g. your internet service provider) that enables you to access newsgroups. If you cannot get some or any newsgroups from your existing news server, use your favourite search engine to search for 'open news servers' - there are lots available.

nick – Nickname, an alias you can give yourself and use when entering a chat channel, rather than using your real name.

Nominet – The official body for registering domain names in the UK, for example web sites whose name ends in .co.uk.

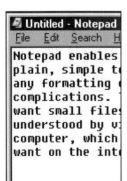

Notepad – The most basic type of word processor which comes with a Windows PC. To find it, click Start, Programs, then Accessories. Its very simplicity makes it ideal for writing and saving HTML pages.

online – The time you spend linked via a modem to the internet. You can keep your phone bill down by reducing online time. The opposite term is offline.

open source software – A type of freely modifiable software, such as Linux. A definition and more information can be found at: www.opensource.org

OS – The operating system in a computer, for example MS DOS (Microsoft Disk Operating System), or Windows 95/98/2000.

packet – The term for any small piece of data sent or received over the internet on your behalf by your internet service provider. It contains your address and the recipient's address. One email message for example may be transmitted as several different packets of information, and reassembled at the other end to recreate the message. The contents of packets can be detected by sniffer software, as used for example by ISPs and government surveillance agencies.

parking – Placing a web domain into storage until it is wanted for public use at a later date.

password – A word or series of letters and numbers that enables a user to access a file, computer or program. A passphrase is a password made by using more than one word.

patch – A small piece of software used to patch up a hole or defect ('bug') in a software program.

Passwords

PC – Personal computer, based on IBM technology. It is distinct from the Apple Macintosh which uses its own different operating system.

PDA – Personal data assistant – a mobile phone, palm top or any other hand-held processor, typically used to access the internet.

PDF – Portable document format, a handy type of file produced using Adobe Acrobat software. It has universal applications for text and graphics.

Pentium – The name of a very popular microprocessor chip in personal computers, manufactured by Intel. The first Pentium IIIs were supplied with secret and unique personal identifiers, which ordinary people surfing the net were unwittingly sending out, enabling persons unknown to construct detailed user profiles. After a storm of protest, Pentium changed the technology so that this identifier could be disabled. If you buy or use a Pentium III computer you should be aware of this risk to your privacy when online.

PGP – Pretty Good Privacy. A proprietary and free method of encoding a message before transmitting it over the internet. With PGP, a message is first compressed then encoded with the help of a pair of keys. Just like the valuables in a locked safe, your message is safe unless a person has access to the right keys. Many governments now want complete access to people's private keys. See: www.pgpi.com

ping – A ping test is used to check the connection speed between one computer and another.

plugin – A type of (usually free and downloadable) software required to add some form of functionality to web page viewing. A well-known example is Macromedia Shockwave, a plugin that enables you to view animations.

PoP – This has two meanings. (1) Point of presence. This refers to the dial-up phone numbers available from your ISP. If your ISP does not have a local point of presence (i.e. local access phone number), then don't sign up - your telephone bill will rocket because you will be charged national phone rates. All the major ISPs have local numbers covering the whole of the country. – (2) Post office protocol. This relates to how your email software retrieves mail from your mail server. When you obtain a SLIP (serial line internet protocol), PPP (point to point protocol) or shell account you usually get a POP account with it.

portal site – Portal means gateway. It is a web site designed to be used as a base from which to explore the internet, or some particular part of it. Yahoo! is a good example of a portal (www.yahoo.com). A portal site includes the one that loads into your browser each time you connect to the internet. It could for example be the front page of your internet service provider.

post, to – The common term used for sending ('posting') messages ('articles') to a newsgroup. Posting messages is very like sending emails, except of course that they are public and everyone can read them. Also, newsgroup postings are archived, and can be read by anyone in the world years later. Because of this, many people feel more comfortable using an 'alias' (made-up name) when posting messages. See: www.deja.com

privacy – Unless you take steps to protect yourself, you have practically no personal privacy online. All your activity online is liable to be logged, analysed and

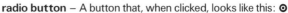

possibly archived by internet organisations, government and surveillance services. You are also leaving a permanent trail of data on your computer. But then, if you have nothing to hide you have nothing to fear... To explore privacy issues worldwide visit the authoritative Electronic Frontier Foundation web site: www.eff.org For the UK see: www.netfreedom.org

program – A series of coded instructions designed to automatically control a computer in carrying out a specific task. Programs are written in special languages including Java, JavaScript VBScript, and ActiveX.

protocol – On the internet, a protocol means a set of technical rules that has been agreed and is used between participating systems. For example, for viewing web pages your computer would use hypertext transfer protocol (http). For downloading and uploading files, it would use file transfer protocol (ftp).

proxy – An intermediate computer or server, used for reasons of security.

Quicktime – A popular free software program from Apple Computers. It is designed to play sounds and images including video clips and animations on both Apple Macs and personal computers.

radio button – A button that, when clicked, looks like this: ⦿

refresh, reload – The refresh or reload button on your browser toolbar tells the web page you are looking at to reload.

register – You may have to give your name, personal details and financial information to some sites before you can continue to use the pages. Site owners may want to produce a mailing list to offer you products and services. Registration is also used to discourage casual traffic. A high proportion of internet users enter fictional details to protect their privacy.

registered user – Someone who has filled out an online form and then been granted permission to access a restricted area of a web site. Access is usually obtained by logging on, typically by entering a password and user name.

remailer – A remailer is an internet service that preserves your privacy by acting as a go-between when you browse or send email messages. An anonymous remailer is simply a computer connected to the internet that can forward an email message to other people after stripping off the header of the messages. Once a message is routed through an anonymous remailer, the recipient of that message, or anyone intercepting it, can no longer identify its origin.

RFC – Request for comment. RFCs are the way that the internet developers propose changes and discuss standards and procedures. See: http://rs.internic.net

RIP – Short for the Regulation of Investigatory Powers Act, which became law in the UK in 2000. It marks the start of draconian surveillance of people's activities on the internet, by routing traffic from internet service providers to a new government agency called GTAC.

RSA – One of the most popular methods of encryption, and used in Netscape browsers. See: www.rsa.com

router – A machine that directs all internet data (packets) from one internet location to another.

rules – The term for message filters in Outlook Express.

script – A script is a set of commands written into the HTML tags of a web page. Script languages such as JavaScript and VBScript work in a similar way to macros in a word processor. Scripts are hidden from view but are executed when you open a page or click a link containing script instructions.

scroll, scroll bar – To scroll means to move part of a page or document into view, or out of view, on the screen. Scrolling is done by using a scrollbar activated by the mouse pointer. Grey scrollbars automatically appear on the right and/or lower edge of the screen if the page contents are too big to fit into view.

QuickTime™

search engine – A search engine is a web site you can use for finding something on the internet. The information-gathering technology variously involves the use of 'bots' (search robots), spiders or crawlers. Popular search engines and internet directories have developed into big web sites and information centres in their own right. There are hundreds of them. Among the best known are AltaVista, Excite, Google, Infoseek, Lycos, Metasearch, Webcrawler and Yahoo!.

secure servers – The hardware and software provided so that people can use their credit cards and leave other details without the risk of others seeing them online. Your browser will flash up a reassuring notice when you are entering a secure site.

secure sockets layer (SSL) – A standard piece of technology which ensures secure financial transactions and data flow over the internet.

security certificate – Information that is used by the SSL protocol to establish a secure connection. Security certificates contain information about who it belongs to, who it was issued by, some form of unique identification, valid dates, and an encrypted fingerprint that can be used to verify the contents of the certificate. In order for an SSL connection to be created both sides must have a valid security certificate.

server – Any computer on a network that provides access and serves information to other computers.

shareware – Software that you can try before you buy. Usually there is some kind of limitation such as an expiry date. To get the registered version, you must pay for the software, typically $20 to $40. A vast amount of shareware is now available online.

Shockwave – A popular piece of software produced by Macromedia, which enables you to view animations and other special effects on web sites. You can download this plugin for free, and in a few minutes, from Macromedia's web site. The effects can be fun, but they slow down the speed at which the pages load into your browser window. See: http://www.macromedia.com

signature file – This is a little text file in which you can place your address details, for adding to email and newsgroup messages. Once you have created a signature file, it is automatically appended to your emails. You can of course delete or edit it at any time.

Slashdot – A leading technology news web site. See: http://slashdot.org

smiley – A form of **emoticon**.

SMTP stands for Simple Mail Transfer Protocol. It is the main protocol (set of rules) used to send and receive electronic mail over the internet. It determines how a program sending mail, and one receiving mail, should interact. The vast majority of email is sent and received by client and server software using SMTP. SMTP was first designed to cope with ASCII text. However, with MIME and other encoding methods you can now attach non-text files to email messages (e.g. images, sound tracks and software programs). SMTP servers route the SMTP messages across the internet to a mail server, such as POP3 or IMAP4. The mail server acts as a message store, from which people can then retrieve their incoming mail.

snail mail – The popular term for the standard postal service involving post-persons, vans, trains, planes, sacks and sorting offices.

sniffer – A program on a computer system (usually an ISP's system) designed to collect information. Sniffers are often used by hackers to harvest passwords and user names, and by surveillance agencies to target wrongdoers.

spam – The popular term for electronic junk mail – unsolicited and unwelcome email messages sent across the internet. There are various forms of spam-busting software which you can now obtain to filter out unwanted email messages.

Glossary of internet terms ·····························

SSL – Secure socket layer, a key part of internet security technology.

subscribe – The term for accessing a newsgroup in order to read and post messages in the newsgroup. There is no charge, and you can subscribe, unsubscribe and resubscribe at will with a click of your mouse. Unless you post a message, no-one in the newsgroup will know that you have subscribed or unsubscribed.

surfing – Slang term for browsing the internet, especially following trails of links on pages across the world wide web.

sysop – Systems operator, someone rather like a moderator for example of a chat room or bulletin board service.

talkers – Chat servers which give users the opportunity to talk to each other. You connect to them, take a 'nickname' and start chatting. Usually, they offer some other features besides just allowing users to talk to each other, including bulletin boards, a virtual world such as a city or building, which you move around in, an opportunity to store some information on yourself, and some games.

TCP/IP – Transmission control protocol/internet protocol, the essential communication rules of the internet.

telnet – Software that allows you to connect across the internet to a remote computer (e.g. a university department or library). You can then access that computer as if you were on a local terminal linked to that system.

template – A pre-designed page which you can adapt in various ways to suit your own needs. Templates are widely used, for example, in popular web authoring packages such as Microsoft Front Page Express.

theme – A term in web page design. A theme describes the general colours and graphics used within a web site. Many themes are available in the form of readymade templates.

thread – An ongoing topic in a Usenet newsgroup or mailing list discussion. The term refers to the original message on a particular topic, and all the replies and other messages which spin off from it. With newsreading software, you can easily 'view thread' and thus read the related messages in a convenient batch.

thumbnail – A small version of a graphic file which, when clicked on screen, expands to a larger size.

top level domain – The last element of a web site's domain name, such as .com or .uk or .net

traceroute – A program that traces the route from your machine to a remote system. It is useful if you need to discover a person's ISP, for example in the case of a spammer.

traffic – The amount of data flowing across the internet, to a particular web site, newsgroup or chat room, or as emails.

trojan horse – A program that seems to perform a useful task but which in fact disguises a malevolent program designed to cause damage to a computer system.

UNIX – This is a computer operating system that has been in use for many years, and still is used in many larger systems. Most ISPs use it.

uploading – The act of copying files from your PC to a server or other PC on the internet, for example when you are publishing your own web pages. It describes the act of copying HTML pages onto the internet via FTP.

URL – Uniform resource locator – the address of each internet page. For instance the URL of Internet Handbooks is: http://www.internet-handbooks.co.uk

Usenet – The collection of well over 80,000 active newsgroups that make up a substantial part of the internet.

Uuencode – This stands for Unix to Unix Encoding. It enables the conversion of files from binary format to ASCII text so that they can be sent over the internet by email.

virtual reality – The presentation of a lifelike scenario in electronic form. It can be

```
⊞  📄 Jack Dupree's
   📄 Vinyl Folk LPs
⊟  📄 HELP! Need LI
   ⊟  📄 Re: HELP! I
      📄 Re: HELF
      📄 Re: HELP! I
⊟  📄 SF Record Sto
      📄 Re: SF Rec
      📄 Re: SF Rec
   📄 Festival de Jaz
   📄 Lady Day/Strai
```

used for gaming, business or educational purposes.

virtual server – A portion of a PC that is used to host your own web domain (if you have one).

virus – A computer program maliciously designed to cause havoc to people's computer files. Viruses can typically be received when downloading program files from the internet, or from copying material from infected disks. Even Word files can be infected through macros. You can protect yourself from the vast majority of them by installing some inexpensive anti-virus software, such as Norton, McAfee or Dr Solomon.

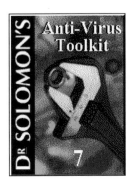

web authoring – Creating HTML pages to upload onto the internet. You will be a web author if you create your own home page for uploading onto the internet.

web – Short for the world wide web. See **WWW** below.

WAP – Wireless Application Protocol, new technology that enables mobile phones and other portable gadgets to access the internet.

web-based chat – A form of internet chat which just uses web pages, and does not require special software like IRC and ICQ. For web-based chat, the settings in your browser must be Java-enabled. Most modern browsers are Java-enabled by default.

web client – Another term for a web browser.

Webcrawler – A popular internet search engine used to find pages relating to specific keywords entered.

webmaster or **webmistress** – Any person who manages a web site.

web page – Any single page of information you can view on the world wide web. A typical web page includes a unique URL (address), headings, text, images, and hyperlinks (usually in the form of graphic icons, or underlined text). One web page usually contains links to lots of other web pages, either within the same web site or elsewhere on the world wide web.

web rings – A network of interlinked web sites that share a common interest. See: www.webring.org

web site – A set of web pages, owned or managed by the same person or organisation, and which are interconnected by hyperlinks.

whois – A network service that allows you to consult a database containing information about someone. A whois query can, for example, help to find the identity of someone who is sending you unwanted email messages.

Windows – The ubiquitous operating system for personal computers developed by Bill Gates and the Microsoft Corporation. The Windows 3.1 version was followed by Windows 95 and 98. Windows 2000 is the latest.

wizard – A feature of many software programs that steps you through its main stages, for example with the use of readymade templates or options.

WWW – The world wide web. Since it began in 1994 this has become the most popular part of the internet. The web is now made up of more than a billion web pages of every imaginable description, typically linking to other pages. Developed by the British computer scientist, Tim Berners-Lee, its growth has been exponential and looks set to continue so.

WYSIWYG – 'What you see is what you get.' If you see it on the screen, then it should look just the same when you print it out.

Yahoo! – Probably the world's most popular internet directory and search engine, valued on Wall Street at billions of dollars: www.yahoo.com

zip/unzip – Many files that you download from the internet will be in compressed format, especially if they are large files. This is to make them quicker to download. These files are said to be zipped or compressed. Unzipping these compressed files means restoring them to their original size. Zip files have the extension '.zip' and are easily created (and unzipped) using WinZip or a similar popular software package. See: www.winzip.com

Index

abuse of email, 42
Acemail, 81
address book, 22
addresses. 11f, 43
agora server, 86
AltaVista email, 77
Anonymizer, 80
anonymous email, 72
antivirus software, 51, 52
AOL (America OnLine), 12, 42
attaching files to emails, 45

backgammon, 65
Bigfoot, 21, 22
blind carbon copies, 26
breaking up large messages, 50
Breathemail, 42
browser, 13
BT Internet, 42

carbon copies, 26
chat rooms, 15
checkers, 65
checking your mail server, 81, 82, 83
chess, 65
CIAC, 57
client software, 13
complaints, 41, 42, 43
composing an email, 16
compressing files, 46, 47, 48, 49
configuring your software, 97
connecting, 17, 19
copies of emails, 26
cryptography, 69
cyber cafes, 77
cypherpunks, 73, 74, 75

decompressing files, 49
Deja, 90
deleting files, 67
deleting messages, 33
Demon Internet, 12, 42
Dial Up Networking, 17, 18, 97
domains, 12
Dr Solomon s Antivirus Toolkit, 53
DUN, 17, 18, 97

Electronic Privacy Information Centre,
    96
email addresses, 11ff, 43
email client, 63, 79
email directories, 21, 22
email discussion groups, 95
email games, 65, 66, 67

email on the move, 76
email programs (clients), 63, 79
email to snail mail, 91
employee emails, 67, 68
encryption, 69
Eudora, 14
Excel, 49
Excite, 78

fax by email, 92
Federal Communication Commission,
    56
file types, 56
file transfer protocol (FTP), 84
files, deleting, 67
files, retrieving by email, 85
filtering emails, 63
    Netscape Messenger, 39, 40, 63
    Outlook Express, 37, 63
finding an email address, 21
folders, using, 35, 36
foreign languages, 93
formatting message text, 27
forwarding a message, 25
F-Prot, 53
Freeserve, 42
FreeUK, 12
Freezip, 48
FTP by email, 84

Games, 65, 66, 67
GIFs, 88

headers, 42, 43
hoaxes, 56, 57
Hotmail, 76, 77, 78
HTML, 14
Hushmail, 78, 79
hyperlinks, 15

identifying sender, 42
images, 29, 49, 88
Inbox folder, 19, 20, 34
incorrect addresses, 43
inserting images, 29
internet mailing lists, 58ff
internet service providers (ISPs), 41, 44

JPEGs, 49
junk email, 40, 41

key servers, 70

list servers, 58

Index . . . .

Liszt, 59, 60
logging on, 17
Lotto, 65

macro viruses, 54, 55
mail bombs, 44
mail server, 15
Mail2Web, 80
mailing lists, 58ff
managing your emails, 33
McAfee antivirus software, 53
message headers, 42, 43
Microsoft Office programs, 54
Mixmasters, 76
multimedia, 14,15
multiple copies, 26

National Computer Security
  Association, 52
netiquette, Appendix C
Netscape Messenger, 14, 20, 23, 30,
  43, 45, 82, 99
Netscape Navigator, 14
networks, email, 9, 52, 65, 68
New Card, 23
news client, 88
news server, 88
newsgroups (Usenet), 88, 89
newsreaders, 36, 37, 63
node, 22
Norton Utilities, 67

offline, working, 15
Outbox folder, 15, 19
Outlook Express, 13, 23, 30, 43, 45, 81,
  83, 98

PaperMail, 91
passphrases, 71
passwords, 17, 19, 68, 71, 78, 80, 81, 98
PDAs, 80
Pegasus, 14
PGP encryption, 69, 70
porn, 67
posting messages in Usenet
  newsgroups, 90
privacy, 68ff
private keys (PGP), 70
pseudo-anonymous remail services, 72
public keys (PGP), 70

quotes in emails, 25

reading email messages, 19
reading newsgroups by email, 89
replying to a message, 24
Rules (Outlook Express), 37, 38, 63

searching the web by email, 87
sending a fax by email, 92
sending and receiving files, 45
servers, 13
sorting messages, 33
sound tracks, 29
spaces in email names, 12
spam, 40, 41
stationery wizard, 27
student emails, 67

T-Mail, 93
Tesco, 42
test messages, 16
toolbar, 20
translation, language, 93
Trash folder (Netscape), 34

UKonline, 42
Usenet by email, 88
usernames, 12, 98, 99

View menu, 20
Virgin Net, 12
viruses, 51

web client (browser), 79
web email access, 76
web-based private email, 78
Winsock connection, 95
WinZip, 47, 48
Word (Microsoft), 49, 54, 55
working offline, 15
workplace emails, 67, 68
writing an email, 16

Yahoo!, 21, 22, 77, 88

Zero Knowledge (ZKS), 75
Zimmerman, Phil, 69
ZipLip, 73

1001 Web Sites for Writers
Nick Daws BSc(Hons)

This handy guide offers what all writers on the net really want – a comprehensive list of web sites relevant to their needs and interests. Each chapter
contains a short introduction followed by an alphabetically arranged list of
web sites relevant to the topic in question. The web sites deal with such topics as grammar, spelling & punctuation, fiction writing, writing for
performance, journalism, research, writers' organisations and communities,
writing resources and software, the writing life, publishers sites, and sites
by and about writers. Each entry summarises what the site offers. The book
includes a list of internet access providers, further reading and reference, and
an alphabetical index.
1 84025 XXX X

Books & Publishing on the Internet
An essential guide for authors, readers, editors, booksellers, librarians & pub-
lishing professionals
Roger Ferneyhough MA(Oxon)

Are you an author, bookseller, publisher or editor? Here is a guide to today's
whole new world of books and publishing information online. The book reviews web sites of every imaginable kind – of publishers, bookstores, writers'
groups, literary agents, book fairs, book distributors, training organisations,
prizes, book-related associations, pressure groups, periodicals and many
more. Whether you are planning to write, edit, publish or distribute a book,
or want to contact a specialist, this is the book for you.
1 84025 332 0

Building a Web Site on the Internet
A practical guide to writing and commissioning web pages
Brendan Murphy BSc(Hons)

The rise in interest in the internet, and especially the word wide web, has
been phenomenal. This book meets the urgent need for all business users
who need an effective internet presence. Written in plain English, it explains
the three main ways of achieving this: create it yourself by writing HTML,
create it yourself by using a popular software package, or create it by hiring
a web development company. Whether your organisation is large or small,
make sure *you* make the right choices for your web site. Brendan Murphy
BSc MBA MBSC teaches HNC in Computing, and lectures for the Open University (Course T171, You, Your computer and the Net). He is a Member of the
British Computer Society, and Institute of Management Information Systems.
1 84025 314 2

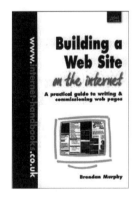

Other Internet Handbooks ....

Careers Guidance on the Internet
An essential guide to careers and vocational guidance resources online
Laurel Alexander MIPD MICG

Are you planning to apply for a new job, or seeking promotion, or looking for new skills? Could you benefit from some vocational guidance, advice or training? Perhaps you are responsible for providing careers guidance to adults or young people? Careers information – like so many other things – is being challenged and revolutionised by the internet. New internet knowledge and skills are urgently needed by every professional working in this vital field. Packed with expert advice, and concise reviews of key web sites, this timely new book will help you take full advantage of some amazing new on-line resources.
1 84025 351 7

Chat & Chat Rooms on the Internet
A practical guide to exploring the live net chat communities
Mark Ray MSc

Whether you're a recent entrant into the internet world, an experienced web user, or even a dedicated operator of an Internet Relay Chat channel, this book provides an in-depth guide to talkers and IRC. It includes detailed snapshots of real online conversations, information on the major networks, and explains how to download and use the tested client software. Written with the help of some of those who make up these new communities, it also looks at how some have organised themselves into virtual democracies, how they are developing, and discusses where all this fantastic new technology may lead. Use this book, and discover how to start using and enjoying these amazing new possibilities for yourself.
1 84025 301 0

Creating a Home Page on the Internet
An illustrated step-by-step guide for beginners
Richard Cochrane BA(Hons) PhD

Have you just started to use the internet? Or perhaps you are still wondering whether to take the plunge? Either way, you will soon be wondering how you can produce and publish web pages of your own, as millions of other individuals have done all over the world. It's easy! Discover how to design a simple but effective home page; see how to add your own artwork and photographs; learn how to add those magic hypertext links that enable you to click effortlessly from one web page to another. Finally, explore how you can actually publish your own home pages in cyberspace, where potentially anyone in the world can pay you a 'visit' and contact you by email.
1 84025 309 6

Discussion Forums on the Internet
A practical step-by-step guide to newsgroups, mailing lists and bulletin board services
Kye Valongo

With a staggering 80,000 different newsgroups now available, Usenet is one of the most established and popular parts of the internet. A vast number of new messages are posted into newsgroups, mailing lists and bulletin board services every day, and millions of people all over the world love to read them. These forums cover every imaginable subject, from local interest to jobs and travel, education, finance, entertainment, raunchy sex and scandal, culture and politics, computing and more. But how do you access them? Are they censored? How do you read the messages, and post messages yourself? Written in plain English, this guide tells you everything you need to know to explore this lively and ever controversial side of the internet.
1 84025 329 0

Education & Training on the Internet
An essential resource for students, teachers, and education providers
Laurel Alexander MIPD MICG

Can't find the information you want? Confused by search engines? Fed up with floods of irrelevant information? Need to save time and money online? Then here is a truly amazing resource, a guide to today's exploding new world of education and training online. Here are web sites of every imaginable kind – for education and training providers, schools, colleges, universities, training centres, professional organisations, resource suppliers, individuals, business organisations and academic institutions. Whether you are planning to study online, or are planning the delivery of online education and training, you will find this a key resource.
1 84025 346 0

Exploring Yahoo! on the Internet
A practical reference guide for internet users everywhere
David Holland ACIB

Yahoo! is one of the two or three most popular web sites on the internet. This practical guide shows you how to get the most out of Yahoo! as an information resource, how to track down over a billion web pages and a vast range of other internet services, using its highly developed local and international search features. But today Yahoo! is much more than just a vast internet directory and search engine. You can use it as a communications tool complete with address book, messaging, email, chat, and greetings services, which you can personalise with your own bookmarks, investment, news and weather updates. You can even get Yahoo! on your mobile phone. The book also explores shopping with Yahoo! including auctions, a business finder, property, classifieds, and communities such as Clubs and Geocities.
1 84025 323 1z

Other Internet Handbooks ....

Finding a Job on the Internet
Amazing new possibilities for jobseekers everywhere
Brendan Murphy BSc (Hons)

Thinking of looking for a new job, or even a change of career? The internet is a really great place to start your job search. In easy steps and plain English, this new Internet handbook explains how to find and use internet web sites and newsgroups to give you what you need. School, college and university leavers will find it a valuable resource for identifying suitable employers and getting expert help with CVs and job applications. The book will also be useful for employers thinking of using the internet for recruitment purposes, and for career and training advisers everywhere.
1 84025 310 X – reprinted

Gardens & Gardening on the Internet
A practical handbook and reference guide to horticulture online
Judith & Graham Lawlor MA

Gardeners are often in need of specific information to help them in their projects, and the internet is proving an amazingly valuable new aid to modern gardening. This new book leads you quickly and painlessly to some amazing new gardening help lines, retail and wholesale suppliers, online clubs and societies, and web sites devoted to such topics as rare plants, water gardens, celebrity gardening, gardening holidays, and horticultural science. The book will be absolutely indispensable for all gardeners with access to the internet.
1 84025 313 4.

Getting Started on the Internet
A practical step-by-step guide for beginners
Kye Valongo

Confused by search engines, worried about email, baffled by browsers? In plain English, this beginner's guide takes you gently step-by-step through all the basics of the internet. It shows you how to obtain free access to the internet, how to set up your computer, how to look for information, and how to send and receive emails. It explains how to explore newsgroups and internet chat, how to protect your privacy online, and even how to create your own home page. Whether you want the internet for use at home, in education or in the workplace, this is the book for you, specially designed to get you up and running with the minimum fuss and bothert.
1 84025 321 5

Graduate Job Hunting on the Internet
A practical illustrated guide for all university and college leavers
Laurel Alexander MIPD MICG

Are you a graduate looking for work? The internet is now by far the easiest way to search for the type of job you want. In a quick and easy format, this book will provide you with everything you need to find the right job in the UK or abroad. Discover how you can keep ahead of the competition by gaining employability skills, where the growth areas of industry and commerce are and how you can always have an income. More than 300 essential sites are reviewed, covering areas such as graduate recruitment agencies, graduate employers and overseas graduate placements. Additional sections provide resources for careers advice, company research, vocational training and job search. Use this book and make sure you are up to speed!
1 84025 361 4

Homes & Property on the Internet
A guide to 1000s of top web sites for buyers, sellers, owners, tenants, sharers, holiday makers & property professionals
Philip Harrison

Here is a guide to today's whole new world of homes and property services online. Here are web sites of every imaginable kind for estate agents, house builders, removal firms, decorators, town planners, architects and surveyors, banks and building societies, home shares, villa owners and renters, and property-related associations, pressure groups, newspapers and magazines. Whether you are planning to move house, or rent a holiday home, or locate property services in the UK or wider afield, this is the book for you – comprehensive and well-indexed to help you find what you want.
1 84025 335 5

Internet Explorer on the Internet
A step-by-step guide to using your browser
Kye Valongo

This book tells you all about Internet Explorer, the world's most popular and powerful browser. In practical steps, it explains how to use it for surfing the internet, how to send and read email messages using Outlook, and how to manage your electronic Address Book. Learn how to store selected web pages as Favourites (bookmarks). Discover how to disable the cookies which web sites secretly place on your computer. Find out how to control or delete the computer files which record your private online activities. If you are using Internet Explorer, or sharing access to a computer at home, college or work, this book will boost both your pleasure and protection when using the internet.
1 84025 334 7

Other Internet Handbooks ....

Law & Lawyers on the Internet
An essential guide and resource for legal practitioners
Stephen Hardy JP LLB PhD

Legal practitioners, law firms, judges, the courts and litigants are now recognising the value of technology in legal research, administration and practice. Following the Woolf Reforms, efficient research and communication will be the key to future legal life. This handbook will meet the needs of solicitors, barristers, law students, public officials, community groups and consumers alike who are seeking guidance on how to access and use the major legal web sites and information systems available to them on the internet. It includes expert site reviews on law associations, law firms, case law and court reporting, European legal institutions, government, legal education and training, publishers, the courts and branches of the law. Don't leave for court without it!
1 84025 345 2

Marketing Your Business on the Internet (2nd edition)
A practical step-by-step guide for all business owners and managers
Sara Edlington

Is your business online? Or perhaps you are still debating whether to take the plunge? For many businesses, the internet will become an essential tool over the next few years, for reaching the vast new online markets for all kinds of goods and services. Written by someone experienced in marketing on the internet from its earliest days, this practical book will show you step-by-step how to make a success of marketing your organisation on the internet. Discover how to find a profitable on-line niche, know which ten essential items to have on your web site, how to keep visitors returning again and again, how to secure valuable on- and off-line publicity for your organisation, and how to build your brand online. The internet is set to create phenomenal new marketing opportunities – make sure you are ready to win your share.
1 84025 364 9 (2nd edition)

Medicine & Health on the Internet
A practical guide to online advice, treatments, doctors and support groups
Sarah Wilkinson

In the last couple of years, thousands of new health and medical web sites have been launched on the internet. Do you want to find out about a specialist treatment or therapy? Do you want to contact a support group or clinician online, or perhaps just get the answer to a simple question? Don't get lost using search engines. Whether you are a patient, relative, carer, doctor, health administrator, medical student or nurse, this book will lead you quickly to all the medical and health resources you need – help lines, support groups, hospitals, clinics and hospices, health insurance and pharmaceutical companies, treatments, suppliers, professional bodies, journals, and more.
1 84025 340 1

Naming a Web Site on the Internet
How to choose, register and protect the right domain name for your web site
Graham Jones BSc(Hons)

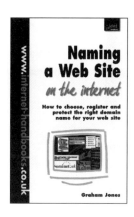

Would you like to obtain a proper domain name for your own web site, for example 'dot.com' or 'dot.co.uk'? Perhaps you have a name in mind, but are not sure how to register it. Do you know the rules which govern the naming of web sites? This valuable handbook explains just how to choose and register your own 'domain name' on the world wide web. The official rules are clearly explained, with lots of practical examples to help you. There are many places you can apply for a domain name and a bewildering array of prices and conditions. This book provides a clear step-by-step guide through the maze. It also explains how to protect your domain names, where to 'host' them, and how to move them from one machine to another. The rush is on – act now to register and protect the names you want.
1 84025 359 2

News & Magazines on the Internet
A practical guide to newspapers, magazines, radio, and other online news and information services
Michael Newman

Here is a truly amazing resource – a handy guide to today's new world of internet newspapers, e-zines, press agencies, newsfeeds, radio and TV broadcasters, and a huge array of other news services online. Discover how to access newspapers and magazines in almost any country. Browse through the *New York Times* or *Wall Street Journal*. Get the latest news and background about politics, sport, finance and entertainment, anywhere from Paris and Berlin to Sydney or Bangkok. Arrange for customised news to be downloaded to your desktop or laptop. Find out what's happening just about anywhere on the planet. Whether you are a media student, teacher, sports fan, pundit, politician or journalist, this book will speed you to all the news and updates you need.
1 84025 342 8

Overseas Job Hunting on the Internet
A practical illustrated guide for everyone seeking employment overseas
Laurel Alexander MIPD MICG

The internet gives you global opportunities for employment and this book will tell you all you need to know to find a great job anywhere in the world. Discover how you can apply for permanent, temporary and contract work. You will find more than 300 top web sites in this book, detailing UK recruitment agencies for overseas work, international recruitment agencies, professional organisations that recruit overseas and companies that recruit overseas. There are also sections on voluntary work overseas, relocation services, embassies and government bodies plus international legislation.
1 84025 366 5

Personal Finance on the Internet
Your complete online guide to savings, investment, loans, mortgages, pensions, insurance and all aspects of personal finance
Graham Jones BSc(Hons)

For many people the internet is now the preferred means of managing their personal finances. But how do you do it? Where can you check out financial products and services on the internet? How secure is it, and what are the risks? Step-by-step this book describes the emerging world of online personal finance. It explains what you need to run your finances on the internet, where to find financial information, managing your bank account online, getting credit via the internet, checking out mortgages online, saving your money online, buying and selling stocks and shares online, arranging your pensions and insurance online, paying taxes, and much more.
1 84025 320 7

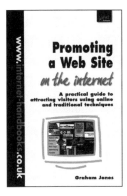

Promoting a Web Site on the Internet
A practical guide to attracting visitors using traditional and online techniques
Graham Jones BSc(Hons)

Do you know how to get your web site listed by the main search engines? Should you pay people to promote your web site? What are banner ads and web rings? This book shows you step-by-step how to plan and carry out the promotion of a new web site. It explains how to use the main search engines and internet indexes, how to use commercial services to get your web site noticed, and how to track down and use various new kinds of cooperative online help. Why not use traditional promotion methods, too? Surprisingly few internet operators use media such as print, mail or radio to promote their web sites. Yet traditional methods reach a wider public and can bring your site to the attention of a huge audience. This book shows you how to maximise both new and traditional promotional techniques, to give your new site the best chance of success.
1 84025 354 1

Protecting Children on the Internet
An effective approach for parents and teachers
Graham Jones BSc(Hons)

Are you concerned that children in your care might view unsuitable material on the internet? Without the right protection, children can easily stumble across pornography, violence, sexism, racism, and other damaging material. This book tells you step-by-step how to make sure that your youngsters are free to get the best from the internet, whilst shielding them from the worst. Using practical examples, it explains how to set up your web browser to protect them, how to use parental controls and filtering software to exclude unwelcome content from your child's screen, and so ensure a positive experience of this powerful new medium.
1 84025 344 4

Shops & Shopping on the Internet
A practical guide to online stores, catalogues, retailers and shopping malls
Kathy Lambert

In the last couple of years, thousands of shops and stores have been launched on the internet. But what are they like? Where can you find your favourite brands and stores? What about deliveries from suppliers in the UK or overseas? Can you safely pay by credit card? Don't get stuck in the internet traffic! This carefully structured book will take you quickly to all the specialist stores, virtual shopping malls, and online catalogues of your choice. You will be able to compare prices, and shop till you drop for books, magazines, music, videos, clothes, holidays, electrical goods, games and toys, wines, and a vast array of other goods and services.
1 84025 327 4

Studying English on the Internet
An A to Z guide to useful electronic resources freely available on the internet
Wendy Shaw

Written by a university researcher, this new guide has been specially collated for the internet user of all levels in the discipline of English. Whether you are a student, teacher, tutor or lecturer, this is the guide for you. It offers a clear and graphical presentation of web sites and electronic resources on the internet for both teaching and research purposes. The A-Z format makes it easy to pick out an author or electronic text centre from the bulleted list. Hundreds of key gateway web sites for English Studies are reviewed in this valuable course companion.
1 84025 317 7

Studying Law on the Interent
How to use the internet for learning and study, exams and career development
Stephen Hardy JP LLB PhD

Are you studying law at college or university, or as a distance learner? Do you have internet access? Computers and the internet are becoming ever more important in both legal learning and practice today. The internet in particular is a place of rich legal resource, for barristers, solicitors, legal executives and officials alike. This handbook meets the needs of law students wanting quick access to the major relevant legal web sites and legal information systems available over the internet. Use this book to expand your knowledge, develop your skills, and greatly improve your career prospects.
1 84025 370 3

Other Internet Handbooks ....

The Internet for Schools
A practical step-by-step guide for teachers, student teachers, parents and governors
Barry Thomas & Richard Williams

This title is aimed at teachers, student teachers, parents and school governors – in fact anyone interested in using the internet in primary and secondary education. The format is entertaining with key points highlighted. Each chapter is free-standing and should take no more than fifteen minutes to read. A major aim is to explain things in clear, non-technical and non-threatening language. There are detailed reviews of many key educational internet sites. The book is UK focused, and contains typical examples and practical tasks that could be undertaken with students.
1 84025 302 9

The Internet for Students
Making the most of the new medium for study and fun
David Holland ACIB

Are you a student needing help with the internet to pursue your studies? Not sure where to start? – then this Internet Handbook is the one for you. It's up to date, full of useful ideas of places to visit on the internet, written in a clear and readable style, with plenty of illustrations and the minimum of jargon. It is the ideal introduction for all students who want to add interest to their studies, and make their finished work stand out, impressing lecturers and future employers alike. The internet is going to bring about enormous changes in modern life. As a student, make sure you are up to speed.
1 84025 306 1 – Reprinted

The Internet for Writers
Using the new medium to research, promote and publish your work
Nick Daws BSc (Hons)

This guide offers all writers with a complete introduction to the internet – how to master the basic skills, and how to use this amazing new medium to create, publish and promote your creative work. Would you like to broaden and speed up your research? Meet fellow writers, editors and publishers through web sites, newsgroups, or chat? Even publish your work on the internet for a potentially enormous new audience? Then this is the book you need, with all the practical starting points to get you going, step by step. The book is a selection of *The UK Good Book Guide.*
1 84025 308 8

Travel & Holidays on the Internet
The amazing new world of online travel services, information, prices, reservations, timetables, bookings and more
Graham Jones BSc (Hons)

Thinking of checking out flights to Europe or America, or booking a package holiday? The internet is the best place to start. In easy steps and plain English, this book explains how to find and use the web to locate the travel and holiday information you need. You can view the insides of hotels, villas and even aeroplanes, quickly compare costs and services, and make your reservations and bookings securely online. All the big holiday and travel companies are now online – from airlines to the major tour operators but you'll be amazed at how much more you'll find with the help of this remarkable book.
1 84025 325 8